OGET
Practice Questions

Mometrix
TEST PREPARATION

DEAR FUTURE EXAM SUCCESS STORY

First of all, **THANK YOU** for purchasing Mometrix study materials!

Second, congratulations! You are one of the few determined test-takers who are committed to doing whatever it takes to excel on your exam. **You have come to the right place.** We developed these practice tests with one goal in mind: to deliver you the best possible approximation of the questions you will see on test day.

Standardized testing is one of the biggest obstacles on your road to success, which only increases the importance of doing well in the high-pressure, high-stakes environment of test day. Your results on this test could have a significant impact on your future, and these practice tests will give you the repetitions you need to build your familiarity and confidence with the test content and format to help you achieve your full potential on test day.

Your success is our success

We would love to hear from you! If you would like to share the story of your exam success or if you have any questions or comments in regard to our products, please contact us at **800-673-8175** or **support@mometrix.com**.

Thanks again for your business and we wish you continued success!

Sincerely,
The Mometrix Test Preparation Team

TABLE OF CONTENTS

Practice Test #1

Reading Test

Questions 1-3 pertain to the following passage:

During difficult economic times, a company may apply to the court for Chapter 11 bankruptcy. This legal filing, a part of the United States bankruptcy law, protects the firm from all creditors while it attempts to reorganize its business and then repay its debts.

By filing Chapter 11, a company will not be closed down due to the outstanding funds it owes to a creditor. While the firm is under the protection of Chapter 11, it will usually make sweeping changes throughout the company. Employees may be laid off or fired, management may be consolidated, buildings may be sold off, and employee benefits may be affected. All changes within the company are designed to return it to profitability, repay creditors, and continue to remain viable.

1. What is the main idea of the passage?
   a. An overview of Chapter 11
   b. Why a company will file for Chapter 11
   c. Legal rules associated with filing Chapter 11
   d. Creditors' rights with Chapter 11

2. When a company is in Chapter 11, executives will make changes mainly:
   a. To work toward solvency
   b. To save money
   c. To ensure their salaries remain intact
   d. To create a smaller company

3. Which statement about the passage is NOT true?
   a. Employee benefits are usually unaffected during Chapter 11.
   b. Chapter 11 is a legal filing.
   c. After a business reorganizes, most debts will be repaid.
   d. Management is often changed during reorganization.

Questions 4-5 pertain to the following passage:

To "take the Fifth" means to refuse to testify against oneself in court. A person cannot be forced to testify in court if that testimony will be self-incriminating. The Fifth Amendment of the Constitution states this basic principle of United States law.

The Miranda decision, a 1966 Supreme Court ruling, states that under the Fifth Amendment, a suspect in police custody has the right to remain silent and to consult an attorney and that anything the person says can be used against him or her in court. This information is recited to suspects before police officers ask them any questions.

Aside from protecting a person in custody and in a court of law, prohibiting self-incrimination ensures that the prosecution is responsible for the burden of proof.

4. According to the passage, which of the following is true?
a. People cannot be forced to testify in court.
b. The Miranda decision protects suspects in police custody.
c. The Miranda decision and "take the fifth" are the same thing.
d. The Fifth Amendment was added in 1966.

5. What is the main purpose of this passage?
a. To explain self-incrimination
b. To discuss our legal system
c. To explain how the Miranda decision came from the Fifth Amendment
d. To discuss suspects' rights

Question 6 pertains to the following passage:

A topographic map is designed to showcase the surface features of a specific land area. These types of maps feature the area's geography and highlight political boundaries, roads, highways, railroads, bodies of water, and some buildings. The maps show the relative positions and elevations of the natural and manmade features of the area.

6. Which of the following would be the best introductory sentence for this passage?
a. Many maps include typographic details.
b. Use a topographic map if you plan to hike in a new area.
c. Comparing two areas is easy with a topographic map.
d. Topographic maps are usually the most inclusive of all map types.

Question 7 pertains to the following passage:

The classic opera *Madame Butterfly* was written by Giacomo Puccini. In the opus, an American naval officer stationed in Japan falls in love with Butterfly, a Japanese woman. He returns to America but promises to come back to marry her. When the soldier does return to Japan three years later, he is accompanied by his American wife. Shocked and humiliated, Butterfly stabs herself. She dies in the soldier's arms as he begs her to forgive him.

7. This passage describes characters' feelings in *Madame Butterfly* as all of the following EXCEPT:
a. Romantic
b. Poignant
c. Crushing
d. Musical

Questions 8-9 pertain to the following passage:

De facto segregation, which literally means segregation "by fact," occurs when a specific socioeconomic group resides in an area with other families of that same demographic. Students living in those areas will typically end up going to neighborhood schools comprised of children of one minority group or one income level. Because it was not considered direct discrimination, de facto segregation was not considered unconstitutional.

De facto segregation was a particularly serious problem in the racially-charged 1960s. Many elementary schools were completely racially segregated, especially in the South, with African Americans attending all-black schools, while white students attended all-white schools. Most people agreed that these schools had vast differences in buildings, materials, and staff, with students from higher-income neighborhoods enjoying an education in what can be described as a higher quality setting than their less-affluent peers at other schools. Although not often discussed, de facto segregation can still be found in our country.

8. According to the passage, which of the following is an example of de facto segregation?
   a. Large schools
   b. Separate schools
   c. Diverse schools
   d. Heterogeneous schools

9. According to the passage, which of the following is true?
   a. De facto segregation happens today.
   b. De facto segregation was never a serious problem.
   c. De facto segregation was a problem only for high income students.
   d. De facto segregation creates equality.

Question 10 pertains to the following passage:

Corrosion is the deterioration of a metal. This decay can be easily seen on pots, pans, jewelry, and silverware. Iron corrodes when it comes into contact with water and oxygen, with the decomposition present as rust. Copper corrodes when it is exposed to the elements, and the decay is present as a green sheen. Silver tarnishes, or corrodes after a period of time, with its deterioration apparent in a dull black covering of the silver surface.

10. Which of the following is NOT stated as a reason for corrosion?
   a. Exposure to elements
   b. Passage of time
   c. Deterioration from heat
   d. Contact with air

3

Question 11 pertains to the following passage:

A market economy, also called a "free economy," is one in which individuals and corporations control the production, marketing, and distribution of goods and services within a society. There is a minimum of government interference in a market economy. Competition between markets keeps prices at a particular level. When prices become too high, consumers will not purchase goods, which forces sellers to adjust prices to a level where consumers will buy.

Market economies have minimal government involvement; this type of economic system still requires some federal regulation. A complete market economy would mean there would be no government regulation or taxation, two components necessary to ensure that the economy keeps running.

11. Which is a true statement about a market economy?
   a. Sellers determine price.
   b. Government determines price.
   c. Competition determines price.
   d. Individuals determine price.

Questions 12-13 pertain to the following passage:

In literature, the problem, usually referred to as the conflict, should be introduced in the early paragraphs of a story and should directly involve the main character. Throughout the story, the main character should seek to determine how the conflict will be resolved. The conflict resolution should not be obvious to the reader; instead, the reader should wonder how things are going to work out and should be connected enough with the main character so that the character's actions matter.

By the end of the story, the main character should have somehow grown or changed, even just a little, from the experience. Stories in which the main character experiences the same lesson over and over again are not as effective as stories in which the character experiences real change. Most readers enjoy thinking about the way a conflict has been resolved and come to their own conclusions after mulling it over for a period of time. When the resolution is simply stated at the end of a story, the reader often ends up with little or nothing to think about.

12. What is the best way to describe conflict?
   a. It is a story situation.
   b. It is a story problem.
   c. It is a resolution.
   d. It is an experience.

13. According to the passage, what is one important element of a good story?
   a. A story in which the lesson learned is narrated by the main character
   b. A story with a problem embedded in the middle
   c. A story with a few different conflicts
   d. A story in which the main character matters to the reader

Questions 14-17 pertain to the following passage:

Journalists often use a recording device to capture the audio transcript of an interview with a subject. The recording device is thought of as a reliable and efficient way to ensure that all important parts of the interview have been archived, which is something that may be complicated for a journalist to do by hand. Besides being difficult to execute quickly, legibly, and efficiently, taking notes by hand can distract the journalist from the interview subject's body language, verbal cues, or other subtle information that can go unnoticed when the journalist is not fully concentrating on the person talking. These missed cues, for example, noticing that the tough-guy interview subject closed his eyes and trembled slightly when he talked about his recently departed mother, could add an interesting perspective to the article.

Relying on a recording device is not without troubles; however, most journalists can quickly relate stories of disappointments they or co-workers have endured due to problems with equipment. For instance, a journalist may not notice low batteries until it is too late. As a result, a portion of an interview can be lost without any way to reclaim it. The machine's volume can be accidentally left too low to hear the subject on later playback, the recorder may be accidentally switched off during the interview, and any number of other unplanned and unexpected electronic malfunctions can occur to sabotage the recording. While recording device problems may not occur often, even a rate of once a year can be extremely problematic for a writer. Some glitches may be unrealized until hours later when the journalist is prepared to work with the recording.

Most experienced journalists do not rely solely on technology when they are interviewing a subject for an article. Instead, as the recording device creates an audio record of the interview, journalists will simultaneously record their own notes by hand. This dual-note method means that most of the time, a wise journalist has two good resources to use as he or she writes the article draft.

14. According to the passage, which of the following is NOT a reason a recording device can be superior to taking notes by hand?

    a.   Note taking can be slow.
    b.   Note taking is unreliable.
    c.   Note taking forces the writer to look away from the subject.
    d.   Note taking can be difficult to read later.

15. Which of the following is NOT an example of body language?

    a.   A quiet answer
    b.   Shocked look
    c.   Wringing hands
    d.   A glance to the side

16. What is the best way journalists can ensure that all interview notes will be available to them when they need them?
   a. Taking notes by hand and also recording them
   b. Bringing recorder batteries regularly
   c. Bringing an extra tape for the recorder
   d. Taping the recorder switch to the *On* position

17. Which title is the best choice for this passage?
   a. The Art of Writing Notes
   b. Conducting an Interview
   c. Tape Recording an Interview
   d. Problems with Interviews

Questions 18-19 pertain to the following passage:

Florence is not the capital of Italy, but from the fourteenth to the sixteenth centuries, it was the heart of the Italian Renaissance. During those years, the city burgeoned with creativity, and great artists and writers whose works came to be considered classics were active in Florence. Michelangelo, Botticelli, Raphael, da Vinci, and the Medici family called the city their home and were among those responsible for its cultural dominance at the time.

Today, tourists still flock to Florence, which is located in the center of Italy on the Arno River, to view the cathedrals, buildings, and other works of architecture that have been preserved largely in excellent condition. Artists of all kinds continue to be attracted to Florence as an inspirational place to practice their craft.

18. What is NOT true about Florence?
   a. It has a rich cultural history.
   b. It is an artistic center.
   c. It is centrally located.
   d. It is the capital of Italy.

19. As it is used in the passage, what does *burgeoned* most nearly mean?
   a. Exploded
   b. Stagnated
   c. Originated
   d. Deteriorated

Question 20 pertains to the following passage:

Scaffolding is a tactical support method used by teachers to assist students so that they are able to successfully accomplish a particular task they would not be able to complete independently. As they scaffold, teachers assess the type and amount of assistance individual students will need to correctly perform a task or respond to a question. The goal is not simply for the student to accomplish the single task, but to internalize the skills needed to complete comparable tasks in the future. Scaffolding may entail cues, comments, or other directives designed to guide the student to a particular response.

20. Which of the following sentences would be a relevant detail to add as the second sentence to the paragraph above?

    a. Scaffolding is individual instruction for the weakest students.

    b. Students will want to use scaffolding methods in all their learning.

    c. Teachers are able to assess students' needs individually when scaffolding.

    d. Scaffolding is done quietly and is unnoticed by many students.

Question 21 pertains to the following passage:

        The U.S. Department of State is a part of the executive branch of the federal government. Commonly referred to as the State Department, it is headed by the Secretary of State who is appointed by the president. The State Department's chief responsibility is United States foreign policy with some of the duties of the department being to confer with foreign government leaders, maintain a good relationship with America's allies, negotiate treaties, and provide aid to countries in need of help after a disaster, war, or other catastrophic occurrence. Such help may be in the form of economic aid or food.

21. According to the passage, what is the main role of the State Department?

    a. Economic aid

    b. Food

    c. Disaster help

    d. Foreign policy

Questions 22-23 pertain to the following passage:

        The concept of gravity intrigued great thinkers even in the earliest of times. Although Aristotle did not accurately determine why objects fall down toward the earth, he did give those researchers who came after him an excellent starting point to move from.

        Galileo was especially influenced by the idea of gravity and its relevance to the world. He was able to show not only that the earth is subject to the pull of gravity, but also that other planets are as well. Galileo confirmed that Earth is not a solitary celestial entity, as there are other large bodies in the solar system that also experienced the same type of gravitational forces. Although parts of his findings were eventually disproven, Galileo's work nevertheless advanced the scientific world's understanding of gravity.

        Taking the ideas of Aristotle and Galileo into account, Isaac Newton continued to study the forces, properties, and principles that rule Earth. His First and Second Laws of Motion were the result of many years of study.

22. Based on the information given, what is a celestial entity?

    a. A body in space

    b. A star grouping

    c. A cosmic alien

    d. A star unit

7

23. Based on the information in the passage, which statement is true?

    a. Galileo's work was proven to be entirely false by later scientists and researchers.
    b. Aristotle and Galileo may have known each other.
    c. The First and Second Laws of Motion were influenced by Galileo's studies.
    d. The earth is the only large body that experiences gravitational pulls.

Question 24 pertains to the following passage:

Within the next decade, many jobs and careers in the STEM (science, technology, engineering, and math) industries will lack adequately trained workers. This problem has been steadily increasing for years. Most big companies have anticipated that the ways in which the decrease in the number of high school graduates choosing a STEM discipline as their major in college will eventually affect the business world. The government is also taking notice of this declining interest in STEM careers. A federally-commissioned study concluded that both the present STEM workforce is aging, and the number of trained applicants to fill those jobs continues to dwindle.

24. Which magazine listed below would be the best fit for this article?

    a. *Parents* magazine
    b. *Teen* magazine
    c. *Teaching PreK-8*
    d. *High School Guidance Counselor*

Question 25 pertains to the following passage:

Conflicts between students occur every day in most schools across the country. Because the conflicts can vary in severity, some do not necessarily require someone in authority to intercede. However, some conflicts can be quite violent and conflict mediation is necessary to arbitrate the problem.

25. Which statement is most likely to appear next in the text?

    a. Some students get hurt in school fights.
    b. Conflict mediation is an effective method of solving school disputes.
    c. Teachers should not have to deal with these problems.
    d. Students get themselves into all kinds of scuffles with their peers.

Questions 26-27 pertain to the following passage:

Today, most everyone with a cell phone has the capability to send and receive text messages. High school students may be the biggest users of this technology. Some parents have had to impose limits on their teen, which oftentimes easily exceeds the three to five hundred text messages allotted to many family plans each month. A flat fee will usually cover this set number of messages, but each additional message may cost twenty or twenty-five cents, an amount that can add up to a staggering figure in a short period of time if a user is texting with wild abandon.

These days, most high school teachers do not permit students to bring cell phones into the classroom. Students may spend more time texting friends rather than pay attention to what is happening in class. Some savvy students have figured out ways to text-message peers inconspicuously and share test answers. Most students would probably agree that there is no reason to have their cell phones with them during the school day; however, most are reluctant to leave their phones in their lockers.

Typing a message into a phone was an unheard of communication method even two decades ago. Today, many young users may not remember life without it.

26. To whom is this passage probably being written?
   a. Those who are in favor of cell phone use in schools
   b. Those who are against cell phone use in schools
   c. The passage is not written to any of these audiences
   d. Those that are against text messaging in school

27. What is the best title for this passage?
   a. Texting Problems
   b. Cell Phones Can Spell Trouble
   c. Texting and Students
   d. Technology Today

Questions 28-29 pertain to the following passage:

Many female marathon runners today may not realize that the Boston Marathon was not always open to women participants. It was not until 1972 that women were welcome to register and officially participate in the race. Before that, some women would attempt to take part in the race in ways that would not divulge their gender. One method was registering with just their first initial and last name. In almost all instances, this type of deception was discovered and the runner was disqualified.

28. Based on what is discussed in the passage, which statement is most likely to be true?
   a. Those that used deception to run in the Boston Marathon were arrested.
   b. There are women alive today who ran as men in the Boston Marathon.
   c. No women ran in the Boston Marathon prior to 1972.
   d. Women runners probably never wanted to race in the Boston Marathon.

29. According to the passage, what best describes the actions most women took so that they could run in the Boston Marathon prior to 1972?
    a. Lie about their gender
    b. Bribe race officials
    c. Run with a male
    d. Threaten officials with lawsuits if they were not granted entry into the race

Question 30 pertains to the following passage:

Writing an online journal is a difficult way to make money. Money is certainly not the goal of every blogger, but a good blog with a large audience can provide an extra income to those who work at it.

If a blogger is able to prove that he or she consistently has a large number of readers who check the blog every few days, the blogger may be able to attract advertisers. These advertisers can be a valuable source of income for the blogger since the online ads will be seen by many people each day.

30. According to the passage, which of the following statements is true?
    a. All blogs make money.
    b. Popular blogs can make money for the blogger.
    c. All bloggers want to earn an income by blogging.
    d. Companies can be easily convinced to advertise on a blog.

Questions 31-34 pertain to the following passage:

Swiss psychologist Carl Jung coined the terms "extrovert" and "introvert" to describe characteristics he identified and classified in people's personalities.

Imagine a restaurant buffet table full of a variety of breakfast food selections. One woman walks over to the table and immediately talks with a chef creating omelets to order. After she orders her omelet, the woman turns and talks with another stranger on her left and then to one on her right. She loudly thanks the chef after he slides the omelet onto her plate. Another woman slips into the buffet line and observes those ahead of her as they lift the lids from the food warmers. She moves through the line silently and then takes her seat with her group.

Jung described an extrovert, such as the woman who talked to people she did not know, as one whose actions are external and apparent. He said that in general, extroverts tend to make friends and establish connections with other people with relative ease. Extroverts are able to assess social situations and make an easy adjustment to being with groups of people. They typically demonstrate an obvious interest in their surroundings and often act without much forethought.

Introverts tend to be more thoughtful than extroverts, and many of their decisions are processed internal without outwardly apparent signs. Introverts will think of what to do in certain situations before they act. Most introverts are more comfortable keeping to themselves than socializing with other people.

31. Which profession is most likely to be chosen by an introvert?
a. A stand-up comedian
b. An event organizer
c. A Master of Ceremonies
d. A painter

32. According to the passage, which is a true statement?
a. Extroverts are bored without people around.
b. Introverts and extroverts do not get along.
c. Extroverts are insensitive people.
d. Introverts like solitary tasks.

33. What do the words "extrovert" and "introvert" describe?
a. Degrees of personal happiness
b. Personality characteristics
c. Demographic classifications
d. Perceived intelligence

34. According to the passage, what is true about an extrovert's actions?
a. They are apparent.
b. They are completely subconscious.
c. They are secretive.
d. They are kind and caring.

Questions 35-40 pertain to the following passage:

Elementary grade students should be able to describe today's weather, as well as the climate of the area in which they live. Depending on their developmental level, students should be able to provide information about whether they live in a dry and hot climate, a tropical climate, or a climate with warm summers and cold winters, often referred to as a continental climate. Students should recognize there are a large number of factors that can affect climate such as: the land and water features of a region, ocean currents, the latitude of an area, and different landforms that may be present.

Students should be aware of how these aspects affect the climate. Elevation is an interesting subject for students to consider. Students should discuss how those areas with a high elevation and close proximity to the equator will experience climatic conditions that are different from those areas with a low elevation that are also located near the equator. Ocean currents can have an effect on a region's climate, and mountain ranges can buffer winds, often causing an area to be warmer than the same area without such wind shields. Teachers should strive to help students develop a clear understanding about how climate and weather are related but have different meanings.

35. Who is the most likely intended audience for this passage?
a. Parents
b. Students
c. Teachers
d. University instructors

11

36. According to the passage above, what is a true statement about students in elementary schools?

    a. All students should be able to talk about the climate of their area and other areas.
    b. All students should be able to describe current weather conditions.
    c. All students should be able to tell how mountains affect climate.
    d. All students should be able to explain how landforms affect climate.

37. Which word best describes seasonal climate, like that of the northeast United States?

    a. Continental
    b. Dry
    c. Hot
    d. Mild

38. According to the passage, what can mountains do to an area's climate?

    a. Block the wind and make it mild
    b. Block the wind and make it warmer
    c. Increase the wind and make it milder
    d. Nothing

39. Of the choices listed, which one does NOT have an effect on an area's climate?

    a. Weather balloons
    b. Ocean currents
    c. An area's elevation
    d. Proximity to the equator

40. Which word best describes the relationship between the words weather and climate?

    a. They are synonyms
    b. They are related words
    c. They are antonyms
    d. They are homophones

Writing Test

Directions: Questions 41-59

In the following section, there are underlined parts to each sentence. One of the underlined parts is incorrectly written. Choose the letter that corresponds with the incorrect underlined part of the sentence. If the entire sentence is correct, choose D for NO ERROR.

41. Nobody could have anticipated the extent of the storm's damage. No error
    A   B   C   D

42. Most people believed that the game would end up being cancelled. No error
    A   B   C   D

43. We gawked at him as he drug the picnic table closer to the grill area. No error
    A   B   C   D

44. Her bicycle basket was loaded down with books and materials to return to the library.
    A   B   C
    No error
    D

45. Her Grandmother ordered monogrammed towels as a gift for the upcoming
    A   B   C
    bridal shower. No error
    D

46. We must ensure that Mike proceeds Ann when the students line up
    A   B   C
    for the graduation ceremony. No error
    D

47. He was discrete in what he said and wrote since he was not yet sure of his role.
    A   B   C
    No error
    D

48. When funding becomes available, we anticipate receiving a new dual-control
    A   B
    car for our driver training program. No error
    C   D

49. Many students yawned, dozed, or talked during the assembly because they were
    A   B
    disinterested in the speaker's message. No error
    C   D

50. Since school vacation is eminent, teachers have difficulty getting students to pay
    A   B
    attention to their lessons during the last few weeks of school. No error
    C   D

51. Marcy believed her parents had ought to have told her she was still grounded
    A   B   C
    for the weekend. No error
    D

52. Fourteen people hanged seven heavy pictures on the interior walls
    A   B   C
    of the lecture room. No error
    D

53. The entire class disagrees with Dr. Olson's views about
    A   B   C
    the future of the mining industry in our area. No error
    D

13

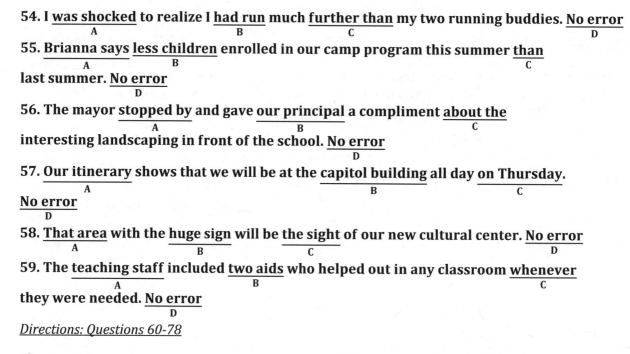

54. I <u>was shocked</u> to realize I <u>had run</u> much <u>further than</u> my two running buddies. <u>No error</u>
    A   B   C   D

55. Brianna says <u>less children</u> enrolled in our camp program this summer <u>than</u>
    A   B   C
last summer. <u>No error</u>
              D

56. The mayor <u>stopped by</u> and gave <u>our principal</u> a compliment <u>about the</u>
              A   B   C
interesting landscaping in front of the school. <u>No error</u>
                                          D

57. Our <u>itinerary</u> shows that we will be at the <u>capitol building</u> all day <u>on Thursday.</u>
         A   B   C
<u>No error</u>
  D

58. <u>That area</u> with the <u>huge sign</u> will be the <u>sight</u> of our new cultural center. <u>No error</u>
    A   B   C   D

59. The teaching staff included <u>two aids</u> who helped out in any classroom <u>whenever</u>
               A   B   C
they were needed. <u>No error</u>
                   D

Directions: Questions 60-78

The upcoming sentences are given to measure your ability to correctly and efficiently convey meaning. When you are choosing your answer, remember that the sentences should utilize conventional written English, including grammar, word selection, conventional sentence structure, and punctuation.

There will be either a section or a complete sentence underlined. Beneath the sentence there are different choices. The first choice (A) will be the same as the underlined section. The remaining choices give different substitutions that could replace the underlined section.

Choose the letter that corresponds with the choice that best conveys the meaning of the original sentence. If the original wording is the best, select answer choice A. If not, choose one of the other choices. The correct answer is the one that keeps the original meaning and makes the sentence the most effective. Make sure your choice makes the sentence understandable without being cumbersome or unclear.

60. When he accepted the award, Mr. Stewart <u>said "that he had never been so wonderfully honored in his life."</u>

    a. said "that he had never been so wonderfully honored in my life."
    b. said that he had never been so wonderfully honored in his life.
    c. said that "he had never been so wonderfully honored in my life."
    d. said that he had "never been so wonderfully honored in my life."

61. Jake <u>borrowed his parents</u> car without permission so they had no way to get to work.

    a. borrowed his parents car
    b. borrowed his parent's car
    c. borrowed his parents' car
    d. borrowed his Parents car

62. **Irregardless of the weather, we will still hold the picnic at the park.**

   a. Irregardless of the weather,
   b. Irregardless because of the weather,
   c. Irregardless of weather
   d. Regardless of the weather,

63. **George sounded excited as he tells his mother about the trip to the factory.**

   a. George sounded excited as he tells his mother
   b. George sounded excited and he tells his mother
   c. George sounds excited as he told his mother
   d. George sounded excited as he told his mother

64. **Feeling weak after running in the long race.**

   a. Feeling weak after running in the long race.
   b. Feeling weak since she had been running in the long race.
   c. Feeling weak on account of running in the long race.
   d. She was feeling weak after running in the long race.

65. **The leaves were raked all day by Sergio and Gina.**

   a. The leaves were raked all day by Sergio and Gina.
   b. The leaves were being raked all day by Sergio and Gina.
   c. Sergio and Gina raked leaves all day.
   d. Leaves were raked all day by Sergio and Gina.

66. **Her hand-sewn dress was beautiful she was proud to wear it to the dinner party.**

   a. Her hand-sewn dress was beautiful she was proud to wear it to the dinner party.
   b. Her hand-sewn dress was beautiful, she was proud to wear it to the dinner party.
   c. Her hand-sewn dress was beautiful; she was proud to wear it to the dinner party.
   d. Her hand-sewn dress was beautiful but she was proud to wear it to the dinner party.

67. **"I hope we find Boots." "He'll be a hungry and tired cat if he spends the night out here,"**

   a. "I hope we find Boots." "He'll be a hungry and tired cat if he spends the night out here,"
   b. "I hope we find Boots." He'll be a hungry and tired cat if he spends the night out here,"
   c. "I hope we find Boots. "He'll be a hungry and tired cat if he spends the night out here,"
   d. "I hope we find Boots. He'll be a hungry and tired cat if he spends the night out here,"

68. **Two of our dogs like to bark at the vacuum cleaner.**

   a. Two of our dogs like to bark
   b. Two of our dog's like to bark
   c. Two of our dogs' like to bark
   d. Two of our dog's like to "bark"

69. **Driving past the park, the new swimming pool was seen.**

   a. the new swimming pool was seen.
   b. he is seeing the new swimming pool.
   c. the new swimming pool was shown.
   d. he saw the new swimming pool.

70. All of the revisions need to be <u>approved by Ellen Jackson and I.</u>

    a. approved by Ellen Jackson and I.
    b. approved by Ellen Jackson and myself.
    c. approved by myself and Ellen Jackson.
    d. approved by Ellen Jackson and me.

71. <u>It was he who wrote the email.</u>

    a. It was he who wrote the email.
    b. It was him who wrote the email.
    c. It was himself who wrote the email.
    d. It was he who had written the email.

72. The <u>scout leader, who had been standing in the road, were</u> hurt in the collision.

    a. scout leader. who had been standing in the road, were
    b. scout leader who had been standing in the road were
    c. scout leader who had been standing in the road were
    d. scout leader, who had been standing in the road, was

73. <u>Using foreign coins is not permitted in our store.</u>

    a. Using foreign coins is not permitted in our store.
    b. Using foreign coins are not permitted in our store.
    c. To be using foreign coins is not permitted in our store.
    d. Using foreign coins, they are not permitted in our store.

74. <u>The turtle trapped himself inside our screened-in porch.</u>

    a. The turtle trapped himself inside our screened-in porch.
    b. The turtle had trapped himself inside our screened-in porch.
    c. The turtle trapped him- or herself inside our screened-in porch.
    d. The turtle trapped itself inside our screened-in porch.

75. <u>"Does your salad taste okay," she asked?</u>

    a. "Does your salad taste okay," she asked?
    b. "Does your salad taste okay," She asked?
    c. "Does your salad taste okay?" she asked.
    d. "Does your salad taste okay." She asked.

76. Most students missed <u>Spanish, Math, and Science today.</u>

    a. Spanish, Math, and Science today.
    b. Spanish, math, and Science today.
    c. Spanish, Math, and science today.
    d. Spanish, math, and science today.

77. She passed <u>the salt and pepper, the butter, and the ketchup to</u> the other table.

    a. the salt and pepper, the butter, and the ketchup to
    b. the salt, and pepper, the butter, and the ketchup to
    c. the salt and pepper, the butter and the ketchup to
    d. the salt and pepper, the butter, and the ketchup, to

78. Now that both of my brothers are married, I have <u>two sister's-in-law.</u>

    a. two sister's-in-law.
    b. two sisters-in-law.
    c. two sisters-in-laws.
    d. two sister-in-laws.

Essay Question

Write 300-600 words on the assigned essay topic. Be sure to write in the correct section of your test booklet. Make sure you stay on topic the entire time you are writing. Write a logical and well-organized paper using specific details to support your main ideas. Use conventional English to write your essay in a clear and precise manner.

Essay topic:

High school administrators are considering outlawing cell phones at school. Despite a rule restricting cell phones to students' lockers during the day, some students still find ways to carry the phones, text-message each other, or use their phones to share test information. Administrators say there is no need for cell phones at school because parents can leave phone messages for their students by calling the office, and students are allowed to use a pay phone or a phone in the office if they need to make a call.

Write an essay discussing your position on the issue of banning cell phones in school.

Math Test

79. What is the probability of spinning a D on the spinner below?

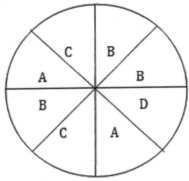

   a. $\frac{1}{8}$

   b. $\frac{1}{7}$

   c. $\frac{3}{8}$

   d. $\frac{6}{7}$

80. Which of the following are supplementary angles?

   a. 101° and 89°
   b. 75° and 75°
   c. 81° and 99°
   d. 90° and 15°

81. A car costs $25,000 plus $675 for tax, title, and license fees. Ari finances the car by putting down $2,500 in cash and taking out a 3-year loan at 4% annual simple interest. What will his monthly payments be?

   a. $649.00
   b. $657.00
   c. $721.00
   d. $743.00

82. What is the value of x in the following equation?

$$15 - x = 78$$

   a. 5.2
   b. 63
   c. -63
   d. -93

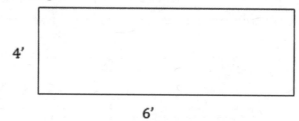

83. Find the area of the rectangle.

4'

6'

    a. 10 ft^2
    b. 12 ft^2
    c. 20 ft^2
    d. 24 ft^2

84. A \$1,000 lottery winner had 35% deducted for taxes. How much was the winning check?

    a. \$300
    b. \$350
    c. \$650
    d. \$965

85. What is the percent increase in cars sold in 2005 when compared to those sold in 2004?

Year	Cars Sold
2002	1,430
2003	1,300
2004	1,580
2005	1,817
2006	1,900

    a. 15%
    b. 18%
    c. 25%
    d. 32%

86. Which of the following choices expresses $\frac{11}{25}$ as a percentage?

    a. 11%
    b. 36%
    c. 40%
    d. 44%

87. Angle ABC measures 150°. What is the measure of angle ABD in the figure below?

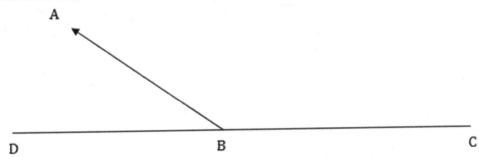

a. 30°
b. 50°
c. 70°
d. It cannot be determined from the information given.

88. The scientific notation for a particular amount is 1.62×10^{-2}. What is this amount in standard form?

a. 162
b. 1.62
c. 0.0162
d. 0.000162

89. A woman wants to park her 15-foot-long car in a garage that is 19 feet long. How far from the front of the garage will the front of her car need to be so that the car is centered on the floor of the garage?

a. 2 feet
b. $2\frac{1}{2}$ feet
c. 3 feet
d. $3\frac{1}{2}$ feet

90. The average highway speed of a charter bus is 65 miles per hour, while a car's average highway speed is 70 miles per hour. If the bus and car both depart from the same place at the same time today, how much farther ahead of the bus is the car after eight hours?

a. 5 miles
b. 15 miles
c. 22 miles
d. 40 miles

91. A man loans his friend $10,000 at 7% simple interest. The friend repays $5,035. How much money does she still owe the man?

a. $5,665
b. $5,465
c. $5,035
d. $4,965

92. Solve for y in the following equation, if $x = -\frac{1}{3}$.

$$y = x + 3$$

a. $y = 2\frac{1}{3}$

b. $y = 2\frac{2}{3}$

c. $y = -2\frac{2}{3}$

d. $y = -3\frac{1}{3}$

93. A hotel's Internet service costs guests $3.00 for the first hour of use and $0.15 for each five minutes over that. A woman uses the service for 3 hours and 10 minutes. What will her Internet charge be?

a. $3.90

b. $5.60

c. $6.90

d. $9.30

94. Arrange the following numbers in order from least to greatest:

0.083	0.017	−0.18	0	1.03	−2.8

a. $-2.8, -0.18, 0, 0.017, 0.083, 1.03$

b. $1.03, 0, 0.017, 0.083, -0.18, -2.8$

c. $0, -2.8, -0.18, 0.083, 0.017, 1.03$

d. $0.017, 0.083, 0, 1.03, -0.18, -2.8$

95. Which pair of angles equals 180°?

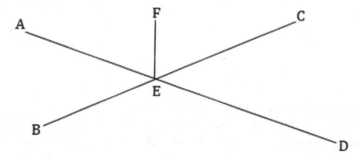

a. $\angle AEF$ and $\angle FEC$

b. $\angle AEB$ and $\angle CED$

c. $\angle AEC$ and $\angle CED$

d. The answer cannot be determined from the information given.

96. Solve for x:

$$4x + 4 = 36$$

a. 5

b. -8

c. 8

d. 11

97. Simplify $8(x + 2) - 7 + 4(x - 7)$.

    a. $5x + 23$
    b. $5x - 23$
    c. $12x - 19$
    d. $12x + 37$

98. What is 40% of 360?

    a. 90
    b. 120
    c. 144
    d. 270

99. Write $\frac{4}{5}$ as a percentage.

    a. 40%
    b. 45%
    c. 60%
    d. 80%

100. Solve for x:

$$\frac{1}{6} \div \frac{3}{8} = x$$

    a. $x = \frac{1}{16}$
    b. $x = \frac{4}{9}$
    c. $x = 2\frac{3}{8}$
    d. $x = 2\frac{1}{3}$

101. A six-sided die is thrown one time. What is the probability of the throw yielding an odd number?

    a. 60%
    b. 50%
    c. 25%
    d. 10%

102. Solve for x:

$$(2x - 3) + 2x = 9$$

    a. 1
    b. -2
    c. 3
    d. -3

103. Express 18% as a decimal.

    a. 0.018
    b. 0.18
    c. 1.8
    d. 0.108

104. Three rectangular gardens, each with an area of 48 square feet, are created on a tract of land. Garden A measures 6 feet by 8 feet; Garden B measures 12 feet by 4 feet; Garden C measures 16 feet by 3 feet. Which garden will require the least amount of fencing to surround it?

    a. Garden A
    b. Garden B
    c. Garden C
    d. All gardens will require the same amount of fencing

105. CF is a straight line. Angle BDF measures 45°. What is the measure of angle BDC?

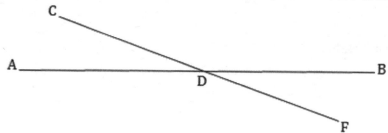

    a. 45°
    b. 135°
    c. 180°
    d. 315°

106. Triangle ABC below is a scalene triangle, not drawn to scale. Which statement is true about side BC?

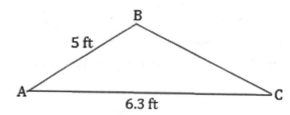

    a. It measures 5 ft.
    b. It measures 6.3 ft.
    c. It does not measure 5 ft or 6.3 ft.
    d. It measures either 5 ft or 6.3 ft.

107. ABC is a right triangle. Angle A measures 30° and Angle B measures 60°. Identify the hypotenuse of the triangle.

    a. Side AB
    b. Side BC
    c. Side AC
    d. Sides AB and AC

108. Jerry and his four friends step onto an elevator with a weight limit of 900 pounds. Jerry weighs 256 pounds. What would the average weight of each of his friends have to be so that the elevator's weight limit is not exceeded?

    a. 128 pounds
    b. 161 pounds
    c. 175 pounds
    d. 200 pounds

109. Which set of numbers shows four factors of 16?

    a. 0, 1, 2, 4
    b. 1, 2, 4, 8
    c. 16, 32, 48, 64
    d. 0, 16, 32, 48

110. A television that regularly costs $400 is offered today at a price reflecting 20% off. When a customer shows a Super Saver card, another 5% is deducted at the register. What does a customer with a Super Saver card pay for the television today?

    a. $380
    b. $375
    c. $300
    d. $304

111. What is the simplest form of $\frac{3}{8} \times \frac{3}{8}$?

    a. $\frac{3}{4}$
    b. $\frac{6}{8}$
    c. $\frac{9}{64}$
    d. $1\frac{1}{8}$

112. Most students can expect to see their grade point averages increase by 8.2% after taking Mrs. Wilson's review class. George's average prior to the class is a 72. What can he expect it to be after taking the class?

    a. 74
    b. 75
    c. 78
    d. 80

113. What is a true statement about the circles below?

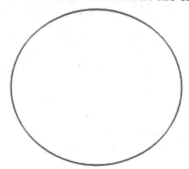 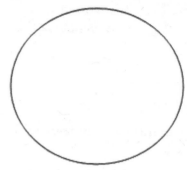

Radius = 8 inches   Radius = 12 inches

a. They are congruent.
b. They are similar.
c. They are neither congruent nor similar.
d. They are equal.

114. Mary's basketball team is losing tonight's game 42-15. Mary scores a three-point shot. How many more three-point shots will someone on her team have to score in order to tie the game?

a. 5
b. 6
c. 7
d. 8

115. Which of the following fractions is 0.18 expressed in its lowest terms?

a. $\dfrac{9}{50}$
b. $\dfrac{18}{100}$
c. $\dfrac{9}{5}$
d. $\dfrac{18}{10}$

116. A can of soda costs 89 cents. A six-pack of the same soda costs $4.50. What is the savings per can when a person buys a six-pack instead of a single can?

a. 5 cents
b. 14 cents
c. 28 cents
d. 84 cents

117. Which of the following is the largest number?

a. 0.004
b. 0.03
c. 0.2
d. 0.400

118. Which number is not a factor of 648?

    a. 3
    b. 2
    c. 7
    d. 8

Answer Key and Explanations

Reading Test

1. A: The main idea of this passage is to provide an overview of Chapter 11 (A). While both paragraphs give information that readers can use to infer why a company would file for Chapter 11 (B), this is not the purpose of the passage. The passage also includes a few details about legal rules associated with Chapter 11 (C), these are only details related to the main idea. The passage does not list any rights that creditors have under Chapter 11 (D), so this also cannot be the main idea.

2. A: The last sentence of the passage states that the changes are intended to restore the company to profitability and repay creditors. These are steps toward achieving solvency (A). While saving money (B) and maintaining salaries (C) may be part of the process of achieving solvency, and are likely goals of the company, they are only parts or steps within executives' overall goal. Creating a smaller company (D) is not mentioned in the passage.

3. A: The passage states that employee benefits can be affected during reorganization (A). Another likely part of reorganization is a change in management (D). The passage states that Chapter 11 is a legal filing (B) used to give a company protected time before it must pay its creditors, meaning that creditors do not receive payment during Chapter 11 proceedings. This also means that most of the company's debts should be repaid once these proceedings are complete (C).

4. B: The passage states that the Miranda decision did establish protections for suspects in police custody (B). The passage only mentions that people cannot be forced to testify if their testimony will be self-incriminating, but it does not say that people, in general, cannot be forced to testify (A). It also clearly says that the Miranda decision was part of a 1966 Supreme Court case (D) and, while the Miranda decision and the Fifth Amendment are related, they are two distinct things (C).

5. A: Each paragraph of this passage refers to aspects of self-incrimination and rights related to self-incrimination (A). The passage only discusses this aspect of the legal system, not the legal system as a whole (B). Similarly, the passage only discusses one right of suspects, not suspects' rights in general (D). The passage only briefly mentions how the Miranda decision came about (C).

6. D: The introductory sentence should provide an overview that is supported by the details that follow. Answer A mentions maps and topographic details, but does not discuss topographic maps. Answers B and C both mention topographic maps, but they also include specific uses for topographic maps that are not discussed in the passage. Answer D specifically mentions topographic maps, is relevant to the details in the rest of the passage, and prepares the reader for the topic and information to follow.

7. D: Although this passage describes an opera, the feelings experienced by the characters would not be considered musical (D). The passage does mention that the American officer falls in love with Butterfly, so it is reasonable to describe the characters' feelings as romantic (A). *Poignant* (B) and *crushing* (C) both refer to feelings of intense emotional distress, which are expressed through both Butterfly and the officer's reactions at the end of the passage. These terms clearly describe the characters' feelings, making *musical* the correct answer.

8. B: The passage uses schools segregated by neighborhood (B) as an example of de facto segregation. Large schools (A) are not necessarily an example of de facto segregation, as the size of the student body alone does not reveal the presence or lack of segregation in the school. Diverse (C)

28

and integrated (D) schools would have students from a variety of backgrounds or demographics, so neither of these would be an example of de facto segregation.

9. A: The end of the passage says "de facto segregation can still be found in our country," meaning that de facto segregation still exists today (A). The passage lists some negative consequences of de facto segregation, showing that it was, and still is, a serious problem (B). According to the passage, during the 1960s, students who lived in low-income neighborhoods suffered the consequences of de facto segregation (C). The passage also states that de facto segregation is based on socioeconomic factors, meaning that de facto segregation does not create equality (D).

10. C: Corrosion due to heat (C) is not mentioned in the passage. According to the passage, contact with oxygen (D) is a cause for iron corrosion, exposure to elements (A) causes copper corrosion, and silver corrosion occurs over time (B).

11. C: The passage notes that "competition between markets keeps prices at a particular level" (C). The passage also states that sellers may adjust prices depending on whether or not consumers purchase goods, and sellers may be corporations or individuals (D), but sellers do not determine prices (A). Market economies also entail very little government involvement, so the government does not determine prices in such an economy (B).

12. B: The passage states that the problem in a story, or the story problem (B), can be called conflict. While the conflict is a type of situation, not every situation in a story (A) is a conflict. Conflicts may be something the character experiences (D), but this does not have to occur through conflicts. Most conflicts have resolutions (C), but conflicts are not resolutions, themselves.

13. D: The passage describes several elements of a good story, including characters with whom readers can connect (D). The passage states that good stories establish conflict early in the story, not in the middle (B) in order to help readers become more invested in the story and the characters' actions. According to the passage, stories where the main character explicitly states what he or she has learned (A) are not as successful as stories that require readers to decide what the lesson is for themselves. The passage also does not discuss whether it is better for stories to have one or multiple conflicts (C).

14. B: The passage mentions that handwriting notes can, on occasion, be more reliable than using a recording device during an interview (B). The passage also mentions that it can be difficult to take notes quickly and legibly. In other words, note taking can be slow (A), and handwritten notes may be difficult to read after the interview (D). The first paragraph states that relying on handwritten notes during an interview can distract journalists and cause them to look away from the person they are interviewing (C).

15. A: In the passage, the first paragraph gives two examples of body language when it describes an interview subject closing his eyes and trembling sightly. This implies that body language is nonverbal, physical cues. A shocked look (B), wringing hands (C), and a glance (D) are all examples of body language, since they are nonverbal, physical actions. Answering a question quietly is not an example of body language because it is a verbal response (A).

16. A: Although the other options are all good practices to ensure that a recorder will work when it is needed, handwriting notes while recording an interview is the best way for journalists to make sure that they have reliable notes from an interview (A). Bringing extra batteries (B) and tapes (C) and ensuring the recorder is on (D) are all wise things to do, but they still may not prevent all malfunctions that may occur when using a recorder.

17. C: "Tape Recording an Interview" (C) is relevant to each section of the passage. The passage includes details related to writing notes (A), but since this is not the main idea, a title focused on this topic is not the best choices. Tape recording an interview is only one part of interviewing, so the title "Conducting an Interview" (B) is too broad for this passage. The passage also only talks about problems that occur when taking notes, not problems with interviews in general, so "Problems with Interviews" (D) is also not the best title.

18. D: The passage clearly states that "Florence is not the capital of Italy" (D). The passage also explains that Florence is at the center of Italy (C). According to the passage, tourists still visit to see the city's architecture, and artists still visit Florence for inspiration. These facts support the statement that Florence is an artistic center (B). The first paragraph of the passage discusses the city's impact and artistic significance during the Italian Renaissance, showing that Florence has a rich cultural history (A).

19. A: *Burgeoned* means "multiplied," or "prospered." In the context of the passage, *exploded* can mean the same thing (A). The other words have meanings that imply different actions. *Stagnated* (B) and *deteriorated* (D) imply that something is decreasing rather than prospering. These do not match the events the passage describes. *Originated* (C) means "started" and does not make sense in the context of the passage.

20. C: Answer C would be the most appropriate as the second sentence in the passage. Answers B and D are both sentences that discuss whether or not students appreciate scaffolding techniques. These would not fit well in the passage because the passage focuses on teachers and scaffolding, not how students feel about scaffolding. Answer A gives a potential definition for scaffolding. However, this sentence does not fit the rest of the information in the passage or the purpose of the passage. Answer C is relevant to all of the information in the passage and flows well with the other sentences.

21. D: The passage clearly states that the State Department's main responsibility is foreign policy (D). Disaster help (C) is a responsibility that may fit within the category of foreign policy, but it is only part of the department's main role. Economic aid (A) and food (B) are resources that the State Department may provide to help countries recover from disasters, but providing these resources is still not the department's main role.

22. A: A "celestial entity" is a body in space (A). The passage says that Earth is not the only celestial entity and then supports this by stating that "there are other large bodies in the solar system." Also, since Earth is a celestial entity, the definition of "celestial entity" must be something that describes Earth. Earth is not a star grouping (B), cosmic alien (C), or a star unit (D), but it is a body in space.

23. C: The passage states that Newton considered the ideas of both Aristotle and Galileo when conducting his own work. This implies that he used those ideas when he came up with his three laws of motion (C). According to the passage, only parts of Galileo's work were proven false (A). There is also no information in the passage about a personal relationship between Aristotle and Galileo (B). The passage states that other celestial entities have gravitational pulls (D).

24. D: The passage discusses an increasing demand for employment in STEM fields and a decreasing interest in these jobs among high school graduates. Of the audiences for each of the listed magazines, high school guidance counselors (D) are the most likely to be interested in this article and find this information useful. Parents (A) and teenagers (B) may be interested in information about STEM careers, but the passage is more relevant to high school guidance counselors who can use this information to guide students as they plan for the future. This information would also not be suited for a teaching magazine since it is not information that would be taught or integrated into classroom instruction (C).

25. B: Answer B is relevant to the passage and expands upon the information in the last sentence. Answer A provides information that is already implied in the last sentence, so it would not add helpful information to the passage. The information in answer C does not build upon the ideas in the passage and shifts the topic. Answer D repeats information that is already stated in the passage and does not expand upon the last idea in the passage.

26. C: The passage provides facts about cell phone text messages and does not appear to address any particular audience. Choices A, B, and D all define an audience based on their opinions concerning using cell phones or texting during school. Cell phone use in schools is only discussed in the second paragraph, so the target audience for the passage is not likely to be any of these.

27. C: Each paragraph in the passage discusses teenagers and texting. Answer C is a title that is relevant to information throughout the passage and summarizes the topic. Answers A and B suggest that the passage is about problems with texting or cell phones. While the passage discusses problems related to texting and cell phones, the last section is not about problems with texting, so these titles are not the best choices. Answer D suggests that the passage is about modern technology. While the passage does discuss modern technology, it specifically focuses on teenagers and their use of modern technology. Answer D is too broad of a title for this passage.

28. B: Some women who ran as men in the Boston Marathon prior to 1972 could still be alive today (B). The passage does not suggest that the women who ran as men were arrested (A). The passage clearly mentions that women ran in the Boston Marathon as men (C). The choice of female runners to run as men implies that they did want to race (D).

29. A: The passage says that women attempted to conceal their gender (A). While it is possible that some women attempted to bribe (B) or threatened to sue race officials (D), neither of these actions are mentioned in the passage. Running with a male in the race (C) is also not mentioned in the passage.

30. B: The passage states that blogs that are popular and have a consistently high number of readers can earn income for the blogger (B). This also means that not all blogs help the blogger make money (A). The passage also states that not every blogger creates a blog to make money (C). However, according to the passage, companies tend to only advertise on blogs that have many frequent visitors, so bloggers may have a difficult time convincing companies to advertise on their blogs (D).

31. D: The passage mentions that introverts tend to be more comfortable by themselves rather than in social situations. A person who chooses a career as a stand-up comedian (A), an event organizer (B), or a Master of Ceremonies (C) will most likely need to interact with others frequently to do his or her job well. A career as a painter is likely to require less social interaction than the other four options (D). According to the information in the passage, a profession as a painter is the most likely of these jobs to be chosen by an introvert.

32. D: Choice D is the only statement that is reasonably supported by the information in the passage, as introverts are more comfortable by themselves and are likely to enjoy solitary tasks. While introverts may tend to be more comfortable alone than in large groups, this does not provide enough evidence to suggest that introverts rarely have friends (A). On the other hand, the passage describes extroverts as having an easy time making friends and being among others, but does not necessarily mean that extroverts are bored without other people around (B). Additionally, the information in the passage explains the differences between introverts and extroverts, but these differences are not enough to support the statement that introverts and extroverts do not get along (C).

33. B: The first paragraph of the passage explains that *extrovert* and *introvert* are terms used to describe personality characteristics (B). These characteristics do not determine an individual's personal happiness (A) or reliably indicate a person's demographic (C) or intelligence (D).

34. A: In the third paragraph of the passage, extroverts' actions are described as "apparent" (A). This means that their actions are often easy for others to perceive, suggesting that they are not secretive (C). While the passage says extroverts often act without forethought, this does not mean that their actions are completely subconscious (B). The passage also does not give any information about whether or not extroverts' actions are done out of kindness and care (D).

35. C: This passage describes what elementary school students should know about weather and climate and how to help students understand and compare and contrast these concepts. Teachers (C) are most likely the target audience for this passage. Parents (A) and students (B) may benefit from this information, as well, but the passage is best suited to inform teachers of things they should keep in mind when teaching students in a classroom setting. This information is not relevant for university-level instruction (D).

36. B: The passage mentions that elementary school students should be able to talk about today's weather and their area's climate (B). A student's ability to discuss other climates (A) and how mountains (C) or other landforms (D) affect climate depends on his or her developmental level, according to the passage. Only the current weather and the climate the student lives in are listed in the passage as things all students should be able to describe.

37. A: The passage defines continental climate as a climate with seasons. The passage suggests that dry (B), hot (C), and mild (D) climates do not have seasons like continental climates do.

38. B: The passage clearly states that a mountain can buffer winds and cause an area to be warmer. Answer A correctly states that mountains block wind, but incorrectly states that this makes nearby areas have a mild climate. Answer C incorrectly states that mountains allow more wind in an area. Answer D is incorrect because the passage does explicitly list some effects mountains can have on a climate.

39. A: The passage mentions the effects that ocean currents (B), elevation (C), and proximity to the equator (D) can have on an area's climate. Weather balloons (A) are simply used to study weather, and they are not mentioned in the passage.

40. B: The passage states that weather and climate have different meanings. They have related meanings, but they are neither synonyms (A) nor antonyms (B). They also do not have similar spellings or pronunciations, so they are not homonyms (C) or homophones (D). However, they are often used within the same basic subject area, so they are related words (B).

Writing Test

41. D: The sentence is correct as it is written.

42. D: The sentence is correct as it is written.

43. B: The past tense of *drag* is *dragged*, not *drug*.

44. D: The sentence is correct as it is written.

45. A: Nouns that name family members are capitalized only when used as a proper noun:

Her grandmother ordered <u>dinner</u>.

I asked Grandmother if she <u>had</u> ordered <u>dinner</u>.

46. B: *Precedes* means "to come before" and is the appropriate choice in this sentence. *Proceeds* means "to carry on."

47. A: *Discrete* means "separate" or "disconnected." *Discreet* means "careful to avoid mistakes" and should be used in this sentence.

48. D: The sentence is correct as it is written.

49. C: *Disinterested* means that a person is impartial or shows no preference. *Uninterested* means "bored" or "showing no interest." *Uninterested* is the appropriate word to use in this sentence.

50. A: *Eminent* means "famous." *Imminent* means "soon." *Imminent* should be used here.

51. B: *Had ought* is considered to be bad grammar. *Ought* should be used alone in this sentence.

52. A: *Hanged* is a word used to describe a method of execution. *Hung* is the past tense of *hang* and should be used here.

53. D: The sentence is correct as written.

54. C: *Further* refers to the degree or extent of something, while *farther* refers to physical distance.

55. B: *Less* is a comparative adjective used with things that cannot be counted or are talked about as a single unit, as in *less afraid* or *less gasoline*. *Fewer* is used when talking about people or about objects and things that are considered in units, as in *fewer students* or *fewer apples*.

56. D: The sentence is correct as it is written.

57. D: The sentence is correct as it is written.

58. C: *Sight* may mean "something that is seen." *Site* refers to a location and is the correct word to use in this sentence.

59. B: *Aid* is a verb meaning "to help." *Aide* means "assistant" and is the appropriate answer choice.

60. B: Quotation marks should enclose only those words that a speaker says. Here, the speaker is not directly quoted.

61. C: Since "they" indicates more than one parent, the plural possessive form of parent should be used here.

62. D: *Irregardless* is not considered to be a conventional English word. *Regardless* is the correct word to use in this sentence.

63. D: Since the sentence begins in the past tense, the rest of the sentence must be in the past tense as well.

64. D: As presented, the original words form a fragment, not a complete sentence with a subject and a verb. The correct response is a sentence and demonstrates better usage than the answer choice before it.

65. C: This sentence is in passive voice. The subject of the sentence should be performing the action rather than having the action done to him/her/it.

66. C: The original sentence is a run-on sentence—two sentences joined together with no punctuation to separate them. A semi-colon must be added after "beautiful."

67. D: Quotation marks are closed when a speaker has finished what he or she is saying, not between sentences of dialogue.

68. A: The sentence is correct as it is written.

69. D: The original sentence is in passive voice and does not provide a subject. Answer choice D provides the best sentence structure.

70. D: The objective case, Ellen Jackson and me, is used here. To test whether *I* or *me* is the correct form to use, remove Ellen Jackson: "All of the revisions need to be approved by *me*."

71. A: The sentence is correct as it is written.

72. D: The subject of the sentence is one person. The singular verb was must be used in order for the subject to agree with the verb.

73. A: The sentence is correct as it is written.

74. D: The gender of most animals in the wild is not known, so *it* is used.

75. C: The question is this part of the sentence: "Does your salad taste okay?" The question mark is laced at the end after "okay." A comma is not added after a question mark that is part of dialogue.

76. D: When written in a sentence, only school subjects that are proper nouns are capitalized.

77. A: The items are part of a list, with salt and pepper considered to be one unit and the other two items as separate units.

78. B: *Sisters-in-law* is the plural of *sister-in-law*.

Math Test

79. A: Experimental probability is a ratio of how many times the spinner will land on the specific letter to the total number of places the spinner can land. In this case, there are eight possible places where the spinner may land. The D is present only in one space, so the probability of landing there is 1 to 8 or $\frac{1}{8}$.

80. C: Supplementary angles are two angles that equal 180° when added together.

81. C: Add $25,000 and $675 to get $25,675. Subtract the down payment of $2,500 to get $23,175. Multiply this by 4% and 3 years to find the interest he will pay: $2,781. Add the interest to the total figure: $23,175 + $2,781 = $25,956. This is the value he will finance for 36 months. Divide by 36 to get $721.

82. C: The equation can be rearranged and simplified as follows:

$$15 - x = 78$$
$$15 - 78 = x$$
$$-63 = x$$

83. D: Recall that area (A) is length (l) times width (w):

$$A = l \times w$$
$$A = 4 \text{ ft} \times 6 \text{ ft}$$
$$A = 24 \text{ ft}^2$$

84. C: Multiply $1,000 by 35% to get the amount deducted: $1,000 \times 35\% = $350.00. Subtract this value from the original amount: $1000 - $350 = $650.

85. A: Use the formula for percent change to solve this problem.

$$\% \ change = \frac{new - old}{old} \times 100\%$$

The "new" value is the number of cars sold in 2005 (1,817). The "old" value is the number of cars sold in 2004 (1,580). Plug these values into the formula and solve:

$$\% \ change = \frac{1,817 - 1,580}{1,580} \times 100\%$$
$$= \frac{237}{1,580} \times 100\%$$
$$= 15\%$$

Because this number is positive, it shows a percent increase of 15%.

86. D: Recall that percent means "per 100," so convert $\frac{11}{25}$ to a percentage by multiplying both the numerator and denominator by 4:

$$\frac{11 \times 4}{25 \times 4} = \frac{44}{100}$$

This means $\frac{11}{25}$ is the same as "44 per 100," or 44%.

87. A: Since they are on a straight line, these two angles are supplementary angles; they add up to 180°, which is the measure of a straight line. Since one angle is 150°, the second angle on this line is:

$$180° - 150° = 30°$$

88. A: To solve, move the decimal left (since the scientific notation has a negative power) 2 places.

89. A: To solve, first figure out how much room is left when her car and the garage are taken into account: 19 feet − 15 feet = 4 feet. To center the car, it would have to be parked 2 feet from the front of the garage.

90. D: Subtract 65 from 70 to find out how much faster the bus is going:

$$70 - 65 = 5 \text{ miles per hour}$$

If the bus is traveling five miles each hour faster than the car, in eight hours it will be 40 miles ahead of the car:

$$5\frac{\text{miles}}{\text{hr}} \times 8 \text{ hr} = 40 \text{ miles}$$

91. A: To begin, calculate the amount of interest: $10,000 × 7% = $700. Add this to the original amount to find out what she owes in total: $10,000 + $700 = $10,700. Subtract what she has paid to find what she still owes: $10,700 − $5,035 = $5,665.

92. B: To solve, place the value of x into the equation:

$$y = -\frac{1}{3} + 3$$
$$y = 2\frac{2}{3}$$

93. C: To solve, first figure out how much she owes over the $3.00 base fee. For each five minutes, she pays an extra 15 cents. For each hour after the first one, she will pay:

$$12 \times 0.15 = \$1.80$$

She has used the service for an extra 2 hours and 10 minutes. Two hours of additional time is:

$$\$1.80 \times 2 = \$3.60$$

Ten minutes of additional time is:

$$\$0.15 \times 2 = \$0.30$$

Adding these two values gives an additional cost of $3.90. Add this to the base fee of $3 for the first hour to get a total bill of $6.90.

94. A: Think of the numbers as they would appear on a number line to place them in the correct order, from the greatest negative number to the greatest positive number.

95. C: Since a straight line has a measure of 180°, choose two angles that, when added together, make up the entire line.

96. C: To solve, isolate the x on one side of the equation.

$$4x = 36 - 4$$
$$4x = 32$$
$$x = 8$$

97. C: To solve, first multiply through the parentheses and then combine like terms:

$$8(x + 2) - 7 + 4(x - 7) = 8x + 16 - 7 + 4x - 28$$
$$= 12x - 19$$

98. C: Multiply 360 by 0.40 to get 144.

99. D: To solve, divide the numerator by the denominator and multiply by 100:

$$\frac{4}{5} = 0.8 \times 100\% = 80\%$$

100. B: To divide fractions, multiply the dividend (the first fraction) by the reciprocal (turn it upside down) of the divisor (the second fraction):

$$\frac{1}{6} \div \frac{3}{8} = \frac{1}{6} \times \frac{8}{3}$$
$$= \frac{8}{18}$$
$$= \frac{4}{9}$$

101. B: A die has a total of six sides, with a different number on each side. Three of these numbers are odd, and three are even. When throwing a die, the probability of rolling an odd number is 3 out of 6 or $\frac{3}{6}$. Reducing the fraction, yields a $\frac{1}{2}$ or 50% chance an odd number will be rolled.

102. C: To solve, rearrange the equation and simplify by combining like terms:

$$(2x - 3) + 2x = 9$$
$$2x - 3 + 2x = 9$$
$$4x - 3 = 9$$
$$4x = 12$$
$$x = 3$$

103. B: To convert a percent into a decimal, move the decimal two places to the left (or divide by 100).

104. A: To solve, find the perimeter (sum of all sides) of each garden:

Garden A: 6 ft by 8 ft rectangle, 6 ft + 8 ft + 6 ft + 8 ft = 28 ft

Garden B: 12 ft by 4 ft rectangle, 12 ft + 4 ft + 12 ft + 4 ft = 32 ft

Garden C: 16 ft by 3 ft rectangle, 16 ft + 3 ft + 16 ft + 3 ft = 38 ft

The smallest perimeter, Garden A, will require the least amount of fencing.

105. B: Since CF is a straight line, its measure is 180°. Since ∠BDF = 45°, then:

$$\angle CDB = 180° - 45° = 135°$$

106. C: A scalene triangle has three sides of different lengths, so side BC could not have a length of 5 feet or 6.3 feet.

107. A: In a right triangle, the side opposite the right angle is the hypotenuse.

108. B: To solve, first subtract Jerry's weight from the total permitted: 900 lb − 256 lb = 644 lb. Divide this by 4 to get the average weight: $\frac{644 \text{ lb}}{4} = 166$ lb

109. B: Factors are the numbers that when multiplied together provide the result. Zero is not a factor of any number. Answer C provides multiples of 16.

110. D: To solve, first subtract the 20% discount ($400 × 0.20 = $80) from the original price:

$$\$400 - \$80 = \$320$$

Then take the 5% discount ($320 × 0.05 = $16) from the total:

$$\$320 - \$16 = \$304$$

111. C: Multiply the numerators by one another to get the new numerator (3 × 3 = 9), and the denominators by one another to get the new denominator (8 × 8 = 64). The result $(\frac{9}{16})$ is in simplest form.

112. C: Multiply George's grade (72) by 8.2% to get 5.904. Add 5.904 to 72 to get 77.904, which rounds to 78.

113. B: Similar figures have the same shape but not necessarily the same size.

114. D: To solve, first add Mary's shot to the score: 42-18. Subtract the figures to see how many points still need to be scored: 42 − 18 = 24. Divide by three, since three points are attained with each shot: 24 ÷ 3 = 8.

115. A: The number 0.18 as a fraction is $\frac{18}{100}$. This can be reduced, by dividing the numerator and denominator by two, to get $\frac{9}{50}$.

116. B: To solve, divide the 6-pack price by 6 to get the single can price: $\frac{\$4.50}{6} = \$0.75$. Subtract $0.75 from $0.89 to find the difference between the prices: $0.89 − $0.75 = $0.14

117. D: A is a number in the thousandths; B is a number in the hundredths; C, D, and E are in tenths. Four-tenths is the largest of these choices.

118. C: To quickly solve, notice that 648 is an even number (divisible by 2), its digits add up to 18 (divisible by 3), and 8 can be divided into the figure.

Practice Test #2

Reading Test

Read the following passage to answer Questions 1-3:

Vocational counseling at the high school level can be invaluable to students, especially those students who may not know the profession they would eventually like to pursue. Good vocational counseling can be very helpful to steer students to the major or career field that works best with their strengths and interests. Not all high schools have vocational counselors on staff, so in many places a school's guidance counselor will be responsible for this job too.

A skilled vocational counselor will first assist students in assessing those areas where they hold their highest interest and abilities. A number of evaluation instruments can be used to evaluate a student's talents, abilities, and personality traits, and often fields a student may not have considered previously will be discovered during this assessment.

1. Which of the following would be a good title for the passage?
  a. An Overview of Vocational Counseling
  b. Why Students Need Vocational Counseling
  c. The Duties of the Vocational Counselor
  d. The Value of the Vocational Counselor

2. According to the passage, the students who benefit most from vocational counseling tend to be:
  a. Those who do not have a chosen profession.
  b. Those who are honest about their interests.
  c. Those who already know their eventual career choice.
  d. Those who have a vocational counselor in their school.

3. The main purpose of the passage is to:
  a. Argue for vocational counseling as a career choice.
  b. Give positive and negative ideas about vocational counseling.
  c. Talk about evaluation instruments.
  d. Tell what vocational counseling can do for students.

Read the following passage to answer Questions 4-5:

Delaying their initial entry to school can cause some children to actually fall behind their peers in learning. Some studies have shown differing early childhood academic achievement results when comparing children from low-income families with those living in middle-income homes. Children from low-income homes tend to begin school with weaker skills than their peers from more advantaged backgrounds. Holding young children back a year before they begin their academic career is sometimes thought to help them mature before beginning school. This practice may actually backfire for some of those children from low-income households. During the additional year at home, these children are thought to be

39

missing opportunities to be cultivating the basic skills in which they could be taking part in a learning environment – skills suggested to be absent in some low-income families.

4. According to the passage, which of the following is true?

a. Children from low-income homes are always weaker in basic skills than children from higher-income homes.
b. Holding children back a year from starting school is always a mistake.
c. Children from high-income homes often begin school with stronger basic skills than children from lower-income homes.
d. Learning at school is preferable to learning at home.

5. What is the main purpose of this passage?

a. To persuade parents to have their kids begin school on time.
b. To explain the problems teachers have with some students.
c. To tell that not all students are starting school with the same basic skills.
d. To explain the disparity in basic skills when kids initially enter school.

Read the following passage to answer Question 6:

Title IX, part of the Higher Education Act, was signed into law by Richard Nixon in 1972. Title IX prohibited colleges and universities accepting Federal funds to discriminate against students based on gender. The law affected athletics by greatly enhancing and increasing the opportunities for women in college sports.

6. Which of the following would be a supporting detail which could add depth to the passage above?

a. The year after the legislation passed, women's participation in sports increased 45% from the year before.
b. Richard Nixon was eventually impeached for his role in the Watergate scandal.
c. The Summer and Winter Olympics were held later that year.
d. Some sports were not interesting to women.

Read the following passage to answer Question 7:

It is important for students at all grade levels to be read aloud to daily at school. Teachers should read aloud for 20 minutes to a half hour and should choose books that encourage students' appreciation of literature, increase their vocabulary, and promote reading as an enjoyable activity. As the teacher reads aloud, he or she should encourage discussion of vocabulary words, story conflict, opinions of certain characters in the story, and predictions about what may happen next in the book.

7. According to the passage, all of the following statements are true EXCEPT:

a. Older students can still benefit from being read aloud to.
b. Student opinions are not as important as discussions about vocabulary words.
c. Predicting what will happen in a story is an important skill for all students.
d. Teachers should ask questions as they read.

The following passage pertains to Questions 8-9:

There are several important rules regarding Five Oaks guests' vehicles. Please ensure you understand and abide by these regulations and indicate such by initializing
5 and returning a copy of this sheet to the front office.

Parking tickets will be issued for those vehicles left in the main lot overnight. If you plan to spend the night at Five Oaks, please
10 ensure you have registered your vehicle, secured and displayed a window label, and are parked in the side lot. We cannot be responsible for tickets issued by the city Police Department.

15 If you are returning to Five Oaks after 11:00 p.m., please use the four-digit pass code to enter the side parking lot. This code changes every 48 hours and should be kept confidential.

20 Thank you for your attention to these rules which are in effect for your safety and the safety of others at Five Oaks.

8. According to the passage, which of the following is an example of going against regulations?
- a. Displaying a window label
- b. Overnight parking in the main lot
- c. Using the pass code
- d. Registering a vehicle

9. According to the passage, which of the following is NOT true?
- a. Five Oaks is a highly secure facility.
- b. The pass code is predictable.
- c. Police patrol the parking lot.
- d. In the past, some guests had cars towed.

Read the following passage to answer Question 10:

The cloze exercise is an important component of students' reading comprehension process. When students read unfamiliar words, they often substitute what they believe to be a synonym to fill in that space in the sentence. The cloze activity asks the student to do essentially the same thing. As they complete a cloze exercise, students call on their prior knowledge and also use context clues within the sentence to fill in a blank as their comprehension of text is assessed.

10. Which of the following was not a reason for a cloze exercise?
- a. Assess spelling
- b. Assess text comprehension
- c. Assess vocabulary
- d. Assess synonym use

Read the following passage to answer Question 11:

The Dawes Act was passed in 1887 and was designed with the goal of turning Native Americans into landowners and farmers. The federal law provided families with one of two options: 160 acres of reservation farm land or double that amount for cattle grazing. The land ownership was believed by the government to be a huge incentive for the Native Americans to take steps toward citizenship and become individuals rather than being dependent on their tribes. As the Native Americans accepted land, their hunting rights on reservation land were restricted. Since hunting and reservation life was an important component of Indian culture, these people were not altogether happy about the turn of events.

11. Which of the following facts is not a reason the government offered land to the Native Americans?
a. To help them become landowners
b. To help them become individuals
c. To help them maintain their rich culture
d. To help begin the citizenship process

Questions 12 and 13 pertain to the following passage:

One component of good story writing is showing and not telling. Showing can be achieved through descriptions of settings, events, and characters' appearances, words, and actions to show what is happening in the story rather than directly telling information as though the story is being narrated by the writer:

It was a cold and rainy morning. The first track meet of the season was scheduled for that day.

Instead of telling the reader information this way, it's often better to show the information. For example, the characters can show information through their words and actions:

Marissa shivered as she stood next to Jessica on the side walk. "Why didn't I bring my coat?" Marissa whined. "It's going to feel like this on the bus, too! And why does it have to rain the morning of our first track meet?"

"I know. I hope it isn't cancelled. I really wanted to see how my meet times were looking. I want to move up to a varsity slot so bad." Jessica huddled close to Marissa and craned her neck to look down the street. She glanced at her watch and frowned.

By having the two characters show the information, the reader has jumped right into the story and learned about the characters in the first few sentences.

12. Which of the following is NOT shown through the characters' words and actions?
a. The bus has not yet arrived to pick up the track team.
b. It is cold outside.
c. Marissa is on the varsity team, while Jessica is not.
d. Marissa and Jessica are friends.

13. What is a true statement about showing and not telling a story?

    a. It is one component of good story writing.
    b. It gives the writer's voice to the story.
    c. It means providing factual information.
    d. It keeps the readers from knowing the characters.

Questions 14-17 pertain to the following passage:

It is important for teachers to model and teach good science lab safety at every opportunity. Students need to be reminded that serious accidents and injuries can occur if they are not attentive to dangers present in the lab. Review practices students will use to take great care in the lab.

Understanding the experiment is an important component of lab safety. Encourage the students to reread the experiment steps a few times and to follow all directions precisely. There should be an adequate supply of safety goggles and students should use them when they are working with any chemicals, glassware, or hot materials. Good practice often dictates having students wear goggles and a lab apron at most times they are working in the science lab.

Students should wear plastic gloves when they are working with chemicals and should be aware of methods of disposing of used gloves. Oven mitts are essential equipment when students are working with heat or flames. Remind students that glass can get hot enough to cause serious burns. Glassware is present throughout a science lab and students should be careful to report broken or chipped glass and to refrain from touching any broken glass. Students should also exercise extreme care when working with knives, scissors, and other sharp and potentially dangerous equipment in the laboratory.

Students with long hair should make sure it is tied back and loose-fitting clothing (e.g., jackets, scarves) should be removed or secured when students are working with fire. Help students appreciate the ease and speed with which flammable materials can become extremely dangerous.

Show students how chemicals and non-reusable lab materials should be correctly disposed of and review the importance of following these guidelines. Provide adequate time at the end of a lab session for students to wash their hands carefully and thoroughly, whether they were wearing gloves or not. Students will be using these basic lab rules throughout their years in a lab – making sure they are using good practices now can ensure their appreciation for the lab and its materials for years to come.

14. Where would this passage most likely appear?

    a. In a student's high school handbook
    b. On a lab equipment label
    c. In the page immediately before each science experiment
    d. In a teacher's science text

15. Which sentence would be the best addition to paragraph 3?

    a. Glass does not change appearance when it is hot.
    b. Some students may misread instructions for an experiment.
    c. Students should complete lab reports after each experiment.
    d. Students can get hurt in a lab.

16. What is the main idea of this passage?

    a. Accidents can happen in the lab.
    b. Good lab practices are important for students to learn.
    c. Teachers are responsible for teaching about lab equipment.
    d. Students can learn quite a bit in the lab.

17. According to the passage, what is a true statement about the lab?

    a. If students are wearing gloves, they may not need to wash their hands.
    b. Broken glass can only be handled by those wearing oven mitts.
    c. Loose-fitting clothing may be unsafe to wear in a lab.
    d. Teachers usually do not wear lab aprons.

Use this passage to answer Questions 18-19:

> Judith Sargent Murray's writings over two hundred years ago provided significant insight into perceptions about the intellectual differences between men and women. During Sargent's lifetime—the 1750s to 1820—men were often thought of as naturally intellectually superior to women. In her writing, Sargent argued that men were not mentally advantaged, they had been educated and that was the reason for their perceived intellectual superiority. Women of those colonial times were largely unschooled.
>
> Sargent contended that women were intellectual equals to men but that they needed the opportunity to be educated. Since they were the primary teachers for their children, Sargent asserted that when women were educated, the entire culture benefited.

18. Based on the facts in the passage, what prediction could you make about children of educated colonial women?

    a. They were smarter than children of uneducated colonial women.
    b. They were just as smart as children of uneducated colonial women.
    c. Their intelligence depended on their father's education level.
    d. They were intellectually equal to their mother.

19. As used in the passage (beginning of paragraph 2), what does the word *contended* most nearly mean?

    a. Terminated
    b. Denied
    c. Concurred
    d. Argued

Use this passage to answer Question 20:

Desalination is a process used to convert sea water to drinkable water. It is used in those areas where there is a shortage of water for drinking, cooking, washing, and bathing. Although desalination works well and is not difficult to do, it is a very expensive process.

To remove the salt from seawater, the water is first heated until it evaporates. The vapor formed during the evaporation process is put into contact with very cold pipes, causing it to turn back into water. The resulting water is free from salt and is drinkable.

20. Which of the following sentences would be a relevant detail to add to the first paragraph above?
 a. In those areas where it is used, desalination is a necessity.
 b. People have probably never heard of desalination.
 c. Most people would be shocked at its cost.
 d. Water is important to daily life.

Read the following passage to answer Question 21:

When students take part in inquiry-based learning, most models prescribe first defining the problem. Students brainstorm inquiry questions to help them learn more about how to resolve the problem. Questions can take a variety of formats and will have varying degrees of usefulness.

Closed-ended questions, those that can be answered with a *yes*, *no*, or other one-word response, tend to provide the least amount of usable data. Open-ended questions, those that can have more than a few correct answers, yield the best information as students work to resolve their identified problem. Students will have to refer to an assortment of resources as they research possible answers to their question.

21. According to the passage, what is the best explanation for not asking close-ended questions?
 a. The teacher has to ask too many of them.
 b. They take too long to create.
 c. They only provide one-word responses.
 d. They are usually misunderstood by students.

Read this passage for answering Questions 22 and 23:

Print newspapers today are in survival mode. The past decade has been an unsettled one for national and local papers as online technology has provided enhanced opportunities for readers to get news. Add our country's current poor economy to the equation and publishers of most large national newspapers don't need to read quarterly figures. They know their circulation continues to fall.

Some newspapers have experimented with charging a fee for access to their online news. Successful subscription-based online newspapers have content that is both unique and valuable. Since many reputable websites offer their news at no charge and it is updated constantly, it is difficult for most newspapers to charge a

45

fee and compete online. Print newspapers must figure out ways to keep their readers loyal, produce revenue, and stay viable in today's changing world. Most newspaper executives know that the window of time to adapt to the market narrows each week.

22. Based on the information given, what is the main reason for the decline of print newspapers?

  a. Rising costs
  b. Poor quality
  c. Changing interests
  d. The internet

23. What does the last sentence of the passage most nearly imply?

  a. All newspapers will fail soon.
  b. Newspapers must act quickly to save the medium.
  c. The economy is not improving.
  d. There are only a few newspapers left.

This passage pertains to Question 24:

During both fission and fusion—two types of nuclear reactions—small quantities of matter are changed into large amounts of energy. Fission involves breaking down. One large nucleus is split into smaller pieces. Nuclear fission is commonly used as a form of energy.

With fusion two light nuclei fuse, or combine, to form one larger nucleus. Unlike fission, fusion has not been used as a reliable and useable alternate form of energy despite it being a powerful nuclear reaction that causes change.

24. What is true about both fission and fusion?

  a. Both are nuclear reactions.
  b. Both involve combining nuclei.
  c. Both are commonly used as an energy source.
  d. Both are unreliable.

Read to answer Question 25:

China's Yangtze River (also known as the Chang) is the longest river in Asia. The Yangtze flows from Tibet, a mountainous region in southwest China, mainly eastward through the center of China, past the city of Shanghai, and finally emptying into the Pacific Ocean. Since the river is so long—about 4,000 miles—the Yangtze is an important transportation and trade route in China.

25. According to the passage, which statement is not true?

  a. All other rivers in Asia must be less than 4,000 miles in length.
  b. Tibet is west of Shanghai.
  c. The Chang River is the longest river in China.
  d. All shipping originates in Tibet.

Passage to read for Questions 26-27:

School vouchers were initially introduced as a solution for those students who were dissatisfied with their zoned public school. Vouchers provided those students with what can best be described as a grant to attend a more highly regarded private school in their area. Some schools in our country are under-performing. Educational assessments do not meet set minimum standards, so school vouchers were seen as one solution for dissatisfied students.

Vouchers do not always resolve the problem. Sometimes students may want to attend a private school but won't have transportation there. Other students may be content in their present underperforming school but are unsure what to do when their classmates leave. Jobs and funding may be lost if enough students leave a school, often eroding the school's performance further.

Since they do not take government funding, many private schools do not have to attain the same standards as public schools. Some private schools may not accept students who are not of a certain academic level and academically challenged students may not be helped at all by vouchers. Private schools often do not have trained teachers and programs in place to work with those students who need remediation or particular types of individualized instruction.

26. According to the passage, what does NOT typically happen when many students leave a particular underperforming school?
   a. New students are admitted at the same rate.
   b. The school population decreases.
   c. Schools lose government funding.
   d. The staff loses jobs.

27. Which student may be most helped by the voucher system?
   a. An academically challenged student
   b. A student happy in his present school
   c. A student with friends at his school
   d. A student who is dissatisfied with his school

Passage to answer Questions 28-29:

As a plunger is depressed, air inside the wide rubber cup is pushed out. This depression action forms a strong, airtight seal around the top of a clogged pipe and the plunger cup is held fast by the air pressure of the user. Continued plunging—pressing down on the plunger—causes an increase in pressure inside the clogged pipe and will usually force out whatever may be causing the clog.

28. What word best describes the organization of this passage?
   a. Inferring
   b. Hypothesizing
   c. Explaining
   d. Modeling

29. As used in the passage, what does the word "depressed" most nearly mean?
 a. Very unhappy
 b. Pushed down
 c. Exhaled hard
 d. Ignored completely

Read to answer Question 30:

 Blogs can be created and written on any subject and even about nothing. Bloggers, as those who write blogs are usually referred, may write a daily dose of wisdom about baseball, childrearing, looking for a job, looking for a boyfriend, or just about what they do every day.

 Many bloggers hope to interest as many readers as they are able to. Serious bloggers, those who update their online journal with regularity, usually hope to gain and hold onto a regular audience.

30. According to the passage, which of the following statements is true?
 a. Some bloggers do not update their blog regularly.
 b. All bloggers want many readers.
 c. Serious bloggers write on serious subjects.
 d. Bloggers are people who read blogs.

Questions 31-34 pertain to the following passage:

 Conflict mediation in many schools requires staff to use specific problem-solving strategies. These tactics are employed with the students involved in the conflict and a teacher or student acting as mediator. A student is a peer mediator and has been trained in conflict resolution. The student mediator uses specific prompts to encourage the involved students to brainstorm ways to resolve the problem. The students are guided to work toward a resolution they both are comfortable with. This meeting of the minds does not always successfully resolve the conflict but is usually considered a positive step to attempt to have students work out problems in a mature and socially acceptable way.

31. According to the passage, who must act as a mediator?
 a. An administrator
 b. Teacher or student
 c. Teacher
 d. Student

32. What is true about conflict mediation?
 a. It always creates a successful resolution.
 b. It rarely works as it is supposed to.
 c. It involves specific strategies.
 d. It solves problems among peer mediators.

33. As used in the passage, what does the word "prompt" most nearly mean?
 a. Suggestion
 b. Punctual
 c. Brainstorm
 d. Rapid

34. What is true of the resolution within a conflict resolution session?

 a. One mediator creates the resolution.
 b. It is one that will work quickly.
 c. It is usually one that will separate the students.
 d. It is one that both parties will agree with.

Passage for answering Questions 35-40:

  Introductions between two professional people who do not know each other involve introducing the lowest-ranked person (often the youngest) to the higher-ranking person. A new teacher aide at a school would be introduced to the principal:

 Ellen, this is Jane Wilson. Jane is working in Pete Richards' classroom and comes to us from Reed Elementary.

  Then introduce the two people in reverse:

 Jane, Ellen Kennedy is our school's principal. She has been with East Side High for the past seven years. Ellen's office is right over there.

  Sometimes a person's name is tricky. The correct pronunciation or the name to be used should be clarified as part of the introduction:

 Karen, I'd like you to meet Angelique DeMarco. Angie will be working as a student teacher for the next three months in Chris Maxwell's first grade classroom.

 George, this is Illiyo Lee. Illiyo goes by the name Ellie. She is visiting our school this week from Tokyo.

  In reverse:

 Ellie, George Smith is our district's curriculum director. George's office is here in our school and I'm sure he will be happy to answer any questions you may have this week.

  Making introductions deliberately and correctly puts everyone at ease. Sometimes the person making the introduction may feel uncomfortable in the role, but those being introduced will be grateful for the time taken to put them at ease.

35. A bank president is being introduced to a new hire. Who is introduced to whom?

 a. The bank president is introduced to the new hire.
 b. The new hire is introduced to the bank president.
 c. The older of the two is introduced to the younger of the two.
 d. The younger of the two is introduced to the older of the two.

36. According to the passage, what usually occurs after one person is introduced to another?

 a. They are introduced in reverse.
 b. They are asked their names.
 c. They are invited to shake hands.
 d. They pronounce their names.

37. According to the passage, what should be done if a person has a difficult name to pronounce?

    a.   Skip that part of her name
    b.   Make a joke about it
    c.   Clarify the correct way to say it
    d.   Use an initial

38. When are formal introductions most often used?

    a.   In all settings
    b.   In a casual setting
    c.   In a professional setting
    d.   In an uncomfortable setting

39. What is the usual goal for introducing two people?

    a.   Make those involved more comfortable
    b.   Review business protocol
    c.   Ensure the highest-ranking person knows everyone
    d.   Ensure the lowest-ranking person knows everyone

40. A city government official and an administrative assistant will be introduced. Who does the introducing?

    a.   The city government official
    b.   The administrative assistant
    c.   A third person
    d.   Both the city government official and the administrative assistant

Writing Test

Directions: Questions 41-59

In the following section, there are underlined parts to each sentence. One of the underlined parts is incorrectly written. Choose the letter that corresponds with the incorrect underlined part of the sentence. If the entire sentence is correct, choose D for NO ERROR.

41. If you <u>put</u> your backpack by the door, you will <u>insure</u> you won't forget to <u>take it</u> home.
     A   B   C
<u>No error</u>
  D

42. Let's write the <u>entire sign</u> in <u>capitol</u> letters so that it <u>can be seen</u> by people who
                  A   B   C
are driving by. <u>No error</u>
            D

43. The <u>student's</u> attitude in math class probably ended up having a <u>negative</u> <u>affect</u>
    A   B   C
on his grade. <u>No error</u>
          D

44. All of the <u>students</u> <u>except</u> Marcus for the <u>free-spirited</u> boy that he is. <u>No error</u>
         A   B   C   D

45. One flu <u>patient</u> had an <u>averse</u> reaction to the drug and <u>had to</u> be hospitalized
          A   B   C
for a week. <u>No error</u>
        D

46. Grandfather said that when <u>he died</u> he wanted <u>his assets</u> divided <u>among</u> his two sons.
                          A   B   C
<u>No error</u>
  D

47. "<u>I hope</u> Mrs. Johnson <u>lets</u> us swim in her <u>pool.</u>" Pam said. <u>No error</u>
  A   B   C   D

48. <u>No one</u> <u>was able</u> to provide a <u>credible</u> explanation for why the vase had simply fallen
   A   B   C
off the shelf. <u>No error</u>
          D

49. The <u>book's table of contents</u> didn't provide <u>much information</u> about the subjects
    A   B   C
covered in each chapter. <u>No error.</u>
               D

50. With Wilson injured and Anderson sick, it is <u>highly unlikely</u> that any school
                        A   B
records will be broken in <u>todays</u> track meet. <u>No error</u>
                  C   D

51. My Mother still likes to talk about <u>the hard time</u> she had with my twin brother <u>and me</u>
    A   B   C
when we were in junior high school. <u>No error</u>
                         D

52. <u>This class of</u> biology students is superior <u>than</u> the one <u>she</u> taught last semester.
    A   B   C
<u>No error</u>
  D

53. <u>Since</u> the baby <u>was born</u> with a <u>congenital</u> heart defect, she immediately
   A   B   C
had to have surgery. <u>No error</u>
              D

54. <u>His uncle</u>, who is a <u>doctor will</u> be joining <u>us</u> on the camping trip. <u>No error</u>
    A   B   C   D

55. The people, <u>who sat in the last row</u>, paid half-price for <u>their seats</u>. <u>No error</u>
                  A   B   C   D

56. The dog ran away <u>just as</u> he had to go to <u>work this</u> was no laughing matter. <u>No error</u>
                  A   B   C   D

57. <u>I am</u> <u>going to go</u> to the museum this afternoon even if <u>their not</u> interested in
  A   B   C
accompanying me. <u>No error</u>
               D

58. <u>Underneath</u> his gruff exterior was a man that was <u>loving and sensitive</u> and who
    A   B   C
had just nursed three sick kittens back to health. <u>No error</u>
                                       D

59. The <u>Frankel's</u> house <u>had been</u> on the market for at least seven months
       A   B
so we were surprised <u>when it was finally sold</u>. <u>No error</u>
                        C   D

Directions: Questions 60-78

The upcoming sentences are given to measure your ability to correctly and efficiently convey meaning. When you are choosing your answer, remember that the sentences should utilize conventional written English, including grammar, word selection, conventional sentence structure, and punctuation.

There will be either a section or a complete sentence underlined. Beneath the sentence there are different choices. The first choice (A) will be the same as the underlined section. The remaining choices give different substitutions that could replace the underlined section.

Choose the letter that corresponds with the choice that best conveys the meaning of the original sentence. If the original wording is the best, select answer choice A. If not, choose one of the other choices. The correct answer is the one that keeps the original meaning and makes the sentence the most effective. Make sure your choice makes the sentence understandable without being cumbersome or unclear.

60. **When questioned, most students <u>said the Math test</u> was too difficult.**
    a.   said the Math test
    b.   say the Math test
    c.   said the math test
    d.   said that the Math test

61. **<u>An only child Jane</u> enjoyed the company of her parents.**
    a.   An only child Jane
    b.   An only child Jane,
    c.   An "only" child, Jane
    d.   An only child, Jane

62. **Many people were not able to figure out <u>where the meeting was at.</u>**
    a.   where the meeting was at
    b.   where the meeting was
    c.   where, the meeting was at
    d.   at where was the meeting

63. **Each student should bring their backpacks** to the assembly.
    a. Each student should bring their backpacks
    b. Each student should bring backpacks
    c. Each student should bring his or her backpack
    d. Each student should bring his backpack

64. If you are not able to take part in class today, **please set down at the side table.**
    a. please set down at the side table.
    b. please set at the side table.
    c. please sit at the side table.
    d. please, sit at the side table.

65. Most of the tickets were sold **the first day they were available.**
    a. the first day they were available.
    b. the first day the tickets were available.
    c. the first day they are available.
    d. the first day they were "available."

66. **A new state high jump record was set by Oscar Smith.**
    a. A new state high jump record was set by Oscar Smith.
    b. A new state high jump record is set by Oscar Smith.
    c. A new state high jump record was being set by Oscar Smith.
    d. Oscar Smith set a new state high jump record.

67. **Whispering so low that no one could hear her.**
    a. Whispering so low that no one could hear her.
    b. Whispering so low no one could hear her.
    c. Whispering low so no one could hear her.
    d. She is whispering so low no one can hear her.

68. **Terry grabs the phone and talked to the police officer.**
    a. Terry grabs the phone and talked to the police officer.
    b. Terry grabbed the phone and talks to the police officer.
    c. Terry grabs the phone and is talking to the police officer.
    d. Terry grabs the phone and talks to the police officer.

69. She didn't realize it would **take so much time to clean the house she was late** for the party.
    a. take so much time to clean the house she was late
    b. take so much time to clean the house, she was late
    c. take so much time to clean the house; she was late
    d. take so much time to clean the house and therefore she was late

70. **"This box can't be used." "The gift is too big,"** Sharon said.
    a. "This box can't be used." "The gift is too big,"
    b. "This box can't be used. The gift is too big."
    c. "This box can't be used." The gift is too big,"
    d. "This box can't be used "The gift is too big,"

71. We were surprised that <u>most people's views involved</u> spending money from the treasury.
    a. most people's views involved
    b. most peoples views involved
    c. most peoples' views involved
    d. most people's views' involved

72. No one in the room seemed <u>to notice Jack and I walk in late.</u>
    a. to notice Jack and I walk in late.
    b. to notice I and Jack I walk in late.
    c. to notice me and Jack walk in late.
    d. to notice Jack and me walk in late.

73. <u>Each of the diamonds are worth over</u> ten thousand dollars.
    a. Each of the diamonds are worth over
    b. Each of the diamonds is worth over
    c. Each of the diamonds are valued at over
    d. All of the diamonds is worth over.

74. <u>She sang beautiful</u> despite her sadness.
    a. She sang beautiful
    b. She sings beautiful
    c. She sings beautifully
    d. She sang beautifully

75. <u>One of our bicycles are</u> missing.
    a. One of our bicycles are
    b. One of our bicycles is
    c. One of our bicycles, are
    d. One, of our bicycles, is

76. <u>"Are you Don Adams," he asked?</u>
    a. "Are you Don Adams," he asked?
    b. "Are you Don Adams?" he asked.
    c. "Are you Don Adams?," he asked.
    d. "Are you Don Adams," He asked?

77. We have enough students for another <u>Science, English, and Health class.</u>
    a. Science, English, and Health class.
    b. Science, English, and health class.
    c. science, English, and health class.
    d. science, english, and health class.

78. <u>We had spaghetti and meatballs, garlic bread, and salad.</u>
    a. We had spaghetti and meatballs, garlic bread, and salad.
    b. We had spaghetti, and meatballs, garlic bread, and salad.
    c. We had, spaghetti and meatballs, garlic bread and salad.
    d. We had spaghetti and meatballs; garlic bread, and salad.

Essay Question

Directions:

Write 300-600 words on the assigned essay topic. Be sure to write in the correct section of your test booklet. Make sure you stay on topic the entire time you are writing. Write a logical and well-organized paper. Use details to support your main ideas. Write in a clear and precise manner. Use conventional English to write your paper.

Essay topic:

Cyber-bullying, intimidating a child using online technology, has become a problem for a small number of children at a middle school in town. Parents of the harassed children have been calling the school and asking administration to help them handle the problem Administrators allege that since the problem is not happening during school hours, it is not something they can get involved with. Even though the perpetrator's identity is not known, one of the affected students is refusing to go to school, citing fear of physical harm.

Write an essay. Discuss your position on the school's role in the cyber-bullying issue.

Math Test

79. What is the probability of spinning a 2 on the first try on the spinner below?

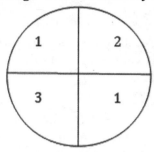

a. $\frac{1}{2}$

b. $\frac{1}{3}$

c. $\frac{1}{4}$

d. $\frac{2}{4}$

80. Which angle measure forms a complementary angle when combined with an angle measure of 48°?

a. 42°

b. 48°

c. 52°

d. 132°

81. Molly borrows $12,000 from a friend. She agrees to make monthly payments to repay the loan in two years along with an additional 10% for interest. What are her monthly payments?

a. $465

b. $550

c. $650

d. $1,010

82. Calculate the value of x in the following equation: $13 + x = 130$.

a. 10

b. 117

c. 143

d. $\frac{13}{130}$

83. Find the area of the rectangle.

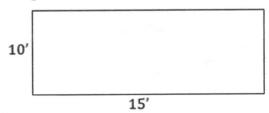

a. 50 ft²
b. 75 ft²
c. 100 ft²
d. 150 ft²

84. 30% of a woman's paycheck goes to health insurance, 15% goes to savings, and 32% goes to taxes. After these deductions, what percentage of the check is remaining?

a. 19%
b. 23%
c. 38%
d. It cannot be determined from the information given.

85. Dale made service calls at a rate of $45/hour last year. He is raising his rates 7% this year. What would a $135.00 bill from the last year cost this year with the increase in rates?

a. $138.00
b. $138.15
c. $142.00
d. $144.45

86. Which of the following choices expresses $\frac{17}{20}$ as a percentage?

a. 85%
b. 80%
c. 63%
d. 32%

87. Angle AEB measures 30°. Angle BEC measures 90°. What is the measure of angle CED in the figure below?

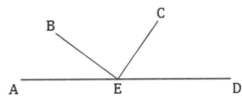

a. 30°
b. 45°
c. 60°
d. 150°

88. The scientific notation for a particular amount is 6.3×10^{-6}. What is that amount in standard form?

    a. 0.0000063
    b. 6,300,000.0
    c. 0.0315
    d. 0.000063

89. A father measures his daughter's height regularly. She is presently 3'8" tall. If she grows 5" in the next year, how much more will she need to grow to be as tall as her 5'1" mother?

    a. 8 inches
    b. 10 inches
    c. 11 inches
    d. 12 inches

90. On Day 1, a driver averages 60 miles per hour for 15 hours of a 2,000-mile car trip. If he maintains this average speed and duration on Day 2, how far will he be from his destination at the end of the day?

    a. 200 miles
    b. 400 miles
    c. 500 miles
    d. 900 miles

91. A woman buys a $125,000 home by putting down 22% of the price and financing the rest. How much of the price has she financed?

    a. $103,000
    b. $97,500
    c. $78,000
    d. $47,500

92. Solve for y in the following equation if $x = -\frac{1}{2}$

$$y = x + 4$$

    a. $y = 2$
    b. $y = 3\frac{1}{2}$
    c. $y = -3\frac{1}{2}$
    d. $y = -4\frac{1}{2}$

93. It costs Jack $7/month for 50 incoming or outgoing text messages and $0.15 for each text message over that. Jack sent 35 text messages this month and received 48. What will his bill be for this month?

    a. $4.20
    b. $4.95
    c. $11.95
    d. $14.20

94. Put the following decimal numbers in order from least to greatest:

$$-1.32 \qquad 0.014 \qquad 0.31 \qquad 0.308 \qquad -0.42 \qquad 0$$

   a. $-0.42, -1.32, 0.31, 0.308, 0, 0.014$
   b. $0.014, 0, 0.308, 0.31, -1.32, -0.42$
   c. $-1.32, -0.42, 0, 0.014, 0.308, 0.31$
   d. $0, -1.32, -0.42, 0.31, 0.308, 0.014$

95. Which pair of angles is equal to 180°?

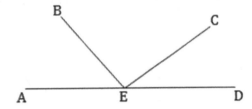

   a. $\angle$AEB and $\angle$BEC
   b. $\angle$CED and $\angle$BEC
   c. $\angle$AEB and $\angle$BED
   d. $\angle$AEC and $\angle$BED

96. What is the value of y in the following equation?

$$4y + 16 = 60$$

   a.   4
   b.   11
   c.   12
   d.   19

97. Simplify: $3(x - 12) - 11 - 3(x - 4)$.

   a. $6x - 35$
   b. $6x + 35$
   c. $6x + 37$
   d. -35

98. What is 25% of 160?

   a.   32
   b.   40
   c.   44
   d.   64

99. Write $\frac{42}{7}$ as a percentage.

   a.   6%
   b.   600%
   c.   60%
   d.   0.06%

100. Solve for x**:** $\left(\frac{2}{5}\right) \div \left(\frac{2}{3}\right) = x$

    a. $x = \frac{1}{4}$

    b. $x = \frac{4}{15}$

    c. $x = 1\frac{2}{3}$

    d. $x = \frac{3}{5}$

101. Of the twenty students in the classroom, half are boys and half are girls. If all students handed in their homework, what is the probability that the top homework sheet belongs to a girl?

    a. 50%

    b. 40%

    c. 30%

    d. 25%

102. Solve for x**:** $(2x - 6) + 4x = 24$

    a. 0

    b. -3

    c. 5

    d. 3

103. What is 22% as a decimal?

    a. 0.22

    b. 0.022

    c. 2.2

    d. 0.202

104. Three rectangular gardens, each with an area of 36 square feet, are created on a tract of land. Garden A measures 4 feet by 9 feet; Garden B measures 12 feet by 3 feet; Garden C measures 18 feet by 2 feet. Which garden will require the most fencing to surround it?

    a. Garden A

    b. Garden B

    c. Garden C

    d. It cannot be determined from the information provided

105. Points A and B are on a straight line. The measure of angle ADC is 45°. What is the measure of angle BDC?

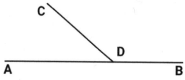

    a. 45°

    b. 135°

    c. 180°

    d. 315°

106. Triangle ABC below is an equilateral triangle, not drawn to scale. Which statement is true about side BC?

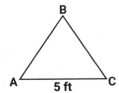

a. It measures less than 5 ft.
b. It measures greater than 5 ft.
c. It measures 2.5 ft.
d. It measures 5 ft.

107. Triangle DEF is a right triangle. Side DE measures 6 feet and side EF measures 8 feet. Which of the following could be the measure of side DF?

a. 8 feet
b. 9 feet
c. 10 feet
d. $\sqrt{14}$ feet

108. Mike is at a Pay-By-The-Ounce salad bar. He places a quarter-pound of blueberries, a half-pound of strawberries, a half-pound of yogurt, and a quarter-pound of walnuts into his bowl. A sign says that the salad bar costs fifteen cents an ounce. How much will Mike's salad cost?

a. $1.80
b. $2.75
c. $3.00
d. $3.60

109. Which shows four factors of 12?

a. 0, 1, 2, 4
b. 1, 2, 3, 4
c. 12, 24, 36, 48
d. 0, 12, 24, 36

110. A pair of $500 earrings is offered today at a 25% discount. If it is your birthday month, the store will take another 5% off of the discounted price. What does Mary pay for the earrings, since this is her birthday month?

a. $250.50
b. $300.00
c. $356.25
d. $400.00

111. What is $\frac{3}{4} \times \frac{4}{5}$, in simplest form?

   a. $\frac{3}{4}$

   b. $\frac{3}{5}$

   c. $\frac{12}{20}$

   d. $\frac{13}{4}$

112. On a typical April day at Mayes Junior High, 8% of the 452 students who attend the school will be absent. About how many students will be absent on April 20?

   a. 36

   b. 38

   c. 40

   d. 44

113. What is a true statement about the rectangles below?

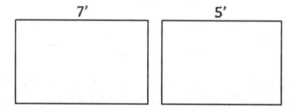

   a. They are congruent.

   b. They are similar.

   c. They are neither congruent nor similar.

   d. They are equal.

114. Tim is paid $5.00 an hour to babysit his neighbor's child. The neighbor says she will give Tim a 20% bonus for today's babysitting if he takes care of their puppy too. Tim works for four hours. How much is he paid for his work today if he takes care of the puppy along with the child?

   a. $20.00

   b. $20.40

   c. $22.00

   d. $24.00

115. Which of the following fractions is in lowest terms?

   a. $\frac{6}{50}$

   b. $\frac{12}{100}$

   c. $\frac{3}{25}$

   d. $\frac{11}{5}$

116. Brenda buys a pair of shoes for $62.00. The next day she sees that the shoes are on sale for 25% off. How much money would Brenda have saved if she had waited a day?

    a. $9.92
    b. $15.50
    c. $25.00
    d. $52.08

117. Which of the following is the largest number?

    a. 0.003
    b. 0.300
    c. 0.1
    d. 0.20

118. Which number is not a factor of 870?

    a. 2
    b. 3
    c. 5
    d. 7

Answer Key and Explanations

Reading Test

1. A: Answer A, "An Overview of Vocational Counseling," most accurately describes the content of the passage, so it is the correct choice. This passage describes the role of the vocational counselor (C) and how vocational counseling benefits students (B). Since the passage covers several aspects of vocational counseling, answers B, C, and D would not be good titles because they are not broad enough to accurately describe the passage.

2. A: The passage describes vocational counseling as a useful tool for students who are not sure what career they want to pursue, or do not have a chosen profession (A). Students who receive vocational counseling will likely have a vocational counselor at their school (D). These students should also be honest about their interests to receive the best results (B). However, these factors do not determine whether or not a student needs or would benefit from vocational counseling. Students who already know what career they wish to pursue will not benefit from vocational counseling as much, as the purpose of this counseling is to help them make this decision (C).

3. D: This passage gives the reader basic information about vocational counseling and how it helps students (D). Answers A and B suggest that the purpose of the passage is to persuade readers to form an opinion or take action regarding vocational counseling. This is not the purpose of the passage, as it is expository. The purpose of the passage is also not to talk about evaluation instruments (C), as they are a detail mentioned only in the second paragraph.

4. C: The passage states that "children from low-income homes tend to begin school with weaker skills than their peers from more advantaged backgrounds," which has the same meaning as answer C. Answers A and B include absolute statements that claim something is true for all students. The passage discusses generalizations, not circumstances that always apply to all students, so these answers are incorrect. The passage does not clearly discuss learning at home, so answer D is also incorrect.

5. D: The main purpose of the passage is to inform readers of factors that can cause a disparity in basic skills in students when they begin attending school (D). While this passage discusses the benefits of allowing children to start school on time, it is not a persuasive passage (A). While the passage mentions the visible disparity in students' basic skills (C), this is a detail discussed in the passage, so it is not the main purpose of the passage. Teachers and their potential problems with students (B) are not mentioned in the passage.

6. A: Answer A describes the impact of Title IX on women's participation in sports. This sentence is relevant to the passage and expands upon the information in the last sentence. Answer B mentions Richard Nixon, who was mentioned in the passage, but this detail is not relevant to the rest of the passage. Answer C includes information related to sports, but is also not relevant to the passage. Answer D discusses some women's lack of interest in sports. While this is relevant to the main idea of the passage, it does not support or build upon the information in the passage.

7. B: The passage states that the teacher should encourage discussions about vocabulary words and students' opinions, meaning that they are of equal importance (B). Predictions about a story's plot (C) is also listed as an important topic teachers should lead students to discuss. According to the passage, teachers can ask questions to encourage these discussions as they read (D). The passage

64

states that reading aloud to students is beneficial for students at any grade level, which includes older students (A).

8. B: In lines 7-8, the passage notes that parking tickets will be issued for vehicles left in the main lot overnight. Overnight guests are instructed to register their vehicles (D) and display a window label (A), so these actions do not violate regulations. The pass code is for guests who need to access Five Oaks after 11:00 p.m., so it is neither an instruction or against regulations (C).

9. B: The passage says that the pass code changes every 48 hours, implying that it is unpredictable and secure (B). The instructions to park in the side lot to avoid receiving a ticket from the city police shows that police are patrolling the facility's parking lot (C). The passage does not mention cars being towed in the past (D), but it does not give evidence that this has not happened.

10. A: Spelling skills (A) are not clearly mentioned in the passage or measurable through the cloze exercise, so answer A is the best choice. The cloze exercise is described as a reading comprehension tool, meaning that it can help evaluate students' text comprehension (B). The passage states that students must use context clues and prior knowledge, which includes vocabulary (C), to fill in blanks during the cloze exercise, so it can also evaluate these skills. The passage also compares the cloze exercise to activities that require students to use synonyms to understand unknown words, which suggests that the cloze exercise also reflects a student's ability to use synonyms (D).

11. C: The passage clearly states that the goal of the Dawes Act was to turn Native Americans into landowners (A) and farmers and that the government hoped this would encourage Native Americans to pursue citizenship (D) and adopt more individualistic lifestyles (B). However, the law deprived many Native Americans of important aspects of their culture, showing that maintaining Native American culture (C) was not a reason the government offered land to Native Americans.

12. C: Jessica says that she wants to be on the varsity team, which shows that she is not on the team. However, the characters do not say or do anything to show whether Marissa is on the varsity team or not (C). Marissa's words show that the characters will be riding a bus, and Jessica's actions show that they are still waiting for the bus to arrive (A). Marissa's words and actions show that it is very cold outside (B). Marissa and Jessica's actions show that they are friends (D), since they talk to each other and stand close together in the cold.

13. A: The introductory sentence of this passage clearly states that showing instead of telling is a component of good story writing (A). Voice in writing (B) is more often achieved through word choice and is not mentioned in the passage. The purpose of showing instead of telling is not to give facts (C). It is instead often used to make descriptions more engaging for the reader. Showing can also help readers know the characters better, as evidenced by the passage (D).

14. D: The passage describes what teachers should do while working with students, therefore, teachers are the audience for this passage (D). Students should be aware of lab safety practices, but this passage is not intended for students, so it would not appear in a student's handbook (A). This passage also applies to a variety of lab situations and materials, so it would not appear on the label for any given lab equipment (B). Also, since this passage covers a variety of information, it would not need to be printed before the instructions for each science experiment (C).

15. A: The third paragraph describes gloves and glassware, so a response about hot glassware (A) would provide an additional detail that is relevant to the information in the paragraph. A sentence about students misreading instructions for an experiment (B) may be relevant to the passage, but it is not directly relevant to this paragraph. Similarly, a sentence stating that students can get hurt in a lab (D) is relevant to the whole passage, but it is also implied throughout the passage and does not strengthen paragraph 3. Whether or not students complete lab reports after experiments (C) is not relevant to this passage.

16. B: Accidents in the lab (A) and instruction over the use of lab equipment (C) are both discussed in the passage. However, these are all details that are included under the main topic of good lab practices that students should learn (B). This is the main idea and applies to each paragraph in the passage, while the other options are only relevant to parts of the passage. While labs are designed for students to learn (D), the passage is about students learning safely rather than students learning a great deal of information.

17. C: As stated in the fourth paragraph, loose-fitting clothing is unsafe to wear when students are working with fire. This means that, in general, loose-fitting clothing may be unsafe to wear in the lab (C). The last paragraph states that students should always wash their hands after completing an experiment, even if they were wearing gloves (A). The passage also states that students should report broken glass and avoid touching it at all (B). The passage does mention that students should wear aprons most of the times they're in the lab, but does not offer any information on whether or not teachers wear aprons in the lab (D).

18. A: According to the passage, one reason Sargent believed women should be educated was because they were the primary teachers for their children. This suggests that an educated mother would educate her child, meaning that children of educated colonial women would most likely be smarter than children of uneducated women (A). This also means that children of educated women would not be intellectually equal to children of uneducated women (B). The passage does not give information to support a generalization comparing a child's education or intelligence to their mother's (D). It also does not mention the influence of the father's education on the child's intelligence (C).

19. D: In the context of the passage, the idea Sargent "contended" seems to be one she suggested, believed, and defended. Based on this context, *argued* (D) is the closest in meaning to *contended*. Neither *terminated* (A), which means ended, or *denied* (B), which means rejected, fit in this sentence because both of these words would suggest that Sargent disagreed or disliked the idea. While using *concurred* (C) would mean that Sargent agreed with the claim, Sargent was making her own claim, meaning that she had no need to agree with another person or idea.

20. A: The necessity of the desalination process (A) is an important detail that is relevant to the information in the first paragraph. The cost of desalination (C) and the importance of usable water (D) are briefly mentioned in the first paragraph, but these sentences do not provide any new information, so they would not expand upon the information in the first paragraph. People's knowledge of desalination (B) is not relevant to the information given in the first paragraph.

21. C: As stated in the passage, closed-ended questions only provide a small amount of usable information (C), so they are not a useful tool in the context of inquiry-based learning. The passage does not discuss questions made by the teacher (A), the amount of time it takes to make questions (B), or how often students understand close-ended questions (D).

22. D: The internet's role in the decline of print newspapers is emphasized throughout the passage (D). Readers' changing interests (C) is mentioned in the passage, but is described as a less impactful factor than the internet. The passage does not discuss the cost of making newspapers (A) or the quality of newspapers (B).

23. B: The last sentence suggests that newspaper executives see a need to make decisions and changes and have a limited amount of time to do so. "Newspapers must act quickly to save the medium" (B) is a reasonable conclusion based on this idea. While the last sentence implies that newspaper executives must act quickly, it does not predict the fate of all newspapers, or suggest that newspapers will fail soon (A). The last sentence does not mention the economy (C) or a scarcity of newspapers (D).

24. A: The passage clearly describes both fission and fusion as nuclear reactions (A). The process of fission involves breaking down matter, while fusion involves combining nuclei (B). The passage also states that fission has been used as a form of energy (C), but fusion has not, and is also not as reliable as fission (D).

25. D: The passage suggests that a great deal of shipping originates in Tibet, but it does not support the statement that all shipping originates there (D). According to the passage, the Yangtze River is almost 4,000 miles long, and is the longest river in Asia. This means that the rest of Asia's rivers must be shorter than 4,000 miles (A), and the Yangtze River must be the longest river in China (C). The passage also says that the river begins in Tibet, in Southwest China, and flows eastward past Shanghai, meaning that Tibet must be west of Shanghai (B).

26. A: The passage states that jobs and funding are at risk of decreasing when many students leave the school at once, so it is not reasonable to assume that new students are admitted at the same rate that former students left (A). Since the school population decreases (B) and government funding (C) and jobs (D) are likely to decrease, schools that experience a large group of students leaving typically become weaker overall.

27. D: According to the passage, the voucher system was designed for students who were not satisfied with their school (D). Students who are happy with their school (B) are not likely to take advantage of the voucher system. The passage states that some private schools may not admit academically challenged students (A), so these students may not always benefit from school vouchers. Whether or not a student has friends at school (C) does not determine whether the student is satisfied with the school, and this is not discussed in the passage.

28. C: The passage describes what happens when a plunger is used to clear a clogged pipe and why this process works. This is best described as an explanation (C). The passage is also simply explaining how plungers work, it is not providing an example or modeling the use of a plunger (D). Inferring (A) means asking a question, and hypothesizing (B) means to propose an unproven idea. The passage does neither of these things.

29. B: "Depressed" is used in the passage to describe how a plunger is pushed down (B) to make it work. "Very unhappy" (A) is not an action, so this answer can be eliminated. The passage also says that when the plunger is depressed, air moves. If the user exhaled on the plunger (C) or ignored it (D), this would not cause the air inside the cup to move.

30. A: The passage mentions that serious bloggers update their blog regularly, implying that bloggers who are not serious about blogging may not do this (A). The passage states that bloggers are people who write blogs (D), and although many bloggers want as many readers as possible, not all bloggers have this goal (B). All bloggers, including serious bloggers, may write about any topic (C), or even a variety of topics.

31. B: In the second sentence, the passage clearly states that a teacher or student may act as mediator (B), so mediators are not limited to being only teachers (C) or only students (D). The passage also does not mention administrators (A).

32. C: The first sentence of the passage states that specific strategies are used in conflict mediation (C). The process of conflict mediation described in the passage includes bringing involved students together so the teacher or peer mediator can lead them through a mature and respectful discussion (D). While second to last sentence explains that conflict mediation does not always lead to a successful resolution (A), the last sentence suggests that conflict mediation often succeeds in achieving other positive results (B).

33. A: The passage states that the mediator uses specific prompts to help students brainstorm solutions. This means the mediator is making suggestions (A) to guide the students' discussion and decision. In this sentence, the word *prompt* must be a noun, so *punctual* (B) and *rapid* (D) are not possible definitions, since they are adjectives. *Brainstorm* (C) is already used in the same sentence as a verb, so it also cannot be the meaning of *prompt*.

34. D: The fourth sentence explains that the resolution should be one that both of the students involved are comfortable with, which implies that both students agree with the resolution (D). While the mediator helps the students reach a resolution, the passage says the mediator's role is to guide the students involved to create a resolution (A). To do this, the mediator talks to the students together, rather than separately (C). The passage does not mention how long the session lasts, so it is unclear whether or not a session works quickly (B).

35. B: The passages states that the lower-ranking person is introduced to the higher-ranking person (B). In this case, the bank president is the higher-ranking person, so the bank president would not be introduced to the new hire (A). Although the lower-ranking person is often younger, this is not always the case, so the order of introductions does not depend on age (C)(D).

36. A: The passage says that after the lower ranking person has been introduced to the higher-ranking person, the two people are introduced in reverse (A). The person introducing the individuals will have already learned the two people's names (B) and how they are pronounced (D). The passage does not mention shaking hands (C).

37. C: The passage states that the correct pronunciation of an unfamiliar name should be clarified during the introduction (C). None of the other options, skipping the difficult part of a person's name (A), joking about a person's name (B), and shortening a person's name to an initial (D), are mentioned in the passage.

38. C: The passage mentions that these types of introductions occur between two professional people (C). These introductions are likely too formal for most casual settings (B), and are certainly not best for all settings (A). One purpose of these introductions is to put individuals at ease, but the passage does not support the idea that these introductions are specifically for uncomfortable conversations (D).

39. A: In the last paragraph, the passage says that introductions help put everyone at ease, or make everyone more comfortable (A). The passage does not discuss reviewing business protocol (B). The passage also only discusses introductions between two people; it does not state that it is important for the highest-ranking (C) or lowest-ranking (D) person to have met everyone.

40. C: The passage describes an introduction process where one person introduces two other people to each other. The ranks of the people being introduced does not matter; a third person (C) will be introducing them. This means that in this situation, neither the city government official (A) or the administrative assistant (B) will introduce themselves.

Writing Test

41. B: The correct word is *ensure*—to make certain by stressing an action taken beforehand.

42. B: "Capitol" refers to the capitol building. The correct word here is "capital," which means an uppercase letter.

43. C: "Affect" means *to influence* whereas "effect" means *end result*.

44. B: "Except" means "instead of." Here, the word should be "accept."

45. B: To be averse to something is to be reluctant to take part in it or to loath it:

She was averse to going to the beach since she was afraid of the big waves.

The word here should be "adverse," which means to have a bad reaction or the opposite reaction that was expected.

46. C: With two people, "between" is used. When speaking of more than two people, "among" is used.

47. C: The sentence is not complete until *said*. Instead of a period after *pool*, a comma should be used.

48. D: The sentence is correct as it is written.

49. D: The sentence is correct as it is written.

50. C: *Today's* tells when which track meet we are referring to. The noun is in the possessive form and needs to have an apostrophe *–s*.

51. A: "Mother" is not capitalized here since it is not being used as a proper noun: I hope my mother won't talk about it. I hope Mother won't talk about it.

52. C: "Superior to" or "smarter than" should be used here. "Superior" is not ordinarily used with "than."

53. D: The sentence is correct as it is written.

54. B: The phrase "who is a doctor" must be included in commas. It is a nonrestrictive (unneeded) clause and it can be removed from the sentence without losing the main idea of the sentence: His uncle will be joining us on the camping trip.

55. A: There should be no commas around this restrictive phrase. The phrase is dependent on the rest of the sentence to create the sentence's meaning.

56. C: This is a run-on sentence. A period should be placed between "work," and "this."

57. C: "They're" should be used here: They are

58. C: Since a person is the subject of the sentence, "who" and not "that" should be used here.

59. A: Since the Frankels are a family, the correct usage would be plural possessive. Thus, the apostrophe should be outside the s.

69

60. C: Only those subjects that are proper nouns (e.g., English, Spanish) are capitalized.

61. D: A comma is used to separate the phrase at the beginning of the sentence from the rest of the sentence to prevent the sentence from being misread.

62. B: The sentence ends in a preposition, which is an example of incorrect grammar.

63. C: The subject refers to the individual (each) student. Students only have one backpack. Response D may be correct if the students are from a group of all males, but the sentence does not indicate this to be so.

64. C: The word "set" is not a synonym for "sit." "Sit" must be used here.

65. A: The sentence is correct as it is written.

66. D: The sentence should begin with Oscar Smith as the subject, putting it in active form.

67. D: This sentence is a fragment – it is not a complete sentence. It needs a subject, which "she" provides.

68. D: The sentence begins in the present tense: *grabs*. The sentence needs to continue in the present tense throughout.

69. C: This is a run-on sentence and the semi-colon is needed to break it into two simple sentences. A period would have also worked to separate the two main ideas here.

70. B: Quotation marks are not closed between sentences. They open at the beginning of the dialogue and close when the person or character is finished speaking.

71. A: The sentence is correct as it is written.

72. D: The nominative case, *Jack and me,* should be used here since they are objects of notice. To test this, take out "Jack and" and read the sentence: to notice *me* walk in late.

73. B: The sentence refers to the singular: *each* diamond. Each is worth over ten thousand dollars.

74. D: *Beautifully*, the adverb form of *beauty* must be used here since it is describing a verb (sang).

75. B: *Is*, the singular form of *to be* must be used here since the sentence refers to just one of the bicycles.

76. B: The first part of the sentence is the question: Are you Don Adams? This part of the sentence is enclosed by quotation marks since it is being said by "him."

77. C: Only subjects that are proper nouns are capitalized, here – just English.

78. A: The sentence is correct as it is written. Spaghetti and meatballs go together as a unit and should not be separated by a comma.

Math Test

79. C: There are four, equally possible places the spinner may land. The digit 2 is only present in one space, so the probability of landing there is 1 out of 4 or $\frac{1}{4}$.

80. A: Complementary angles are two angles that equal 90° when added together:

$$90° - 48° = 42°$$

81. B: Multiply $12,000 by 10% to get $1,200. Add these figures together to find out the total amount. Molly will repay $13,200. Divide this by 24 months to find out the monthly payments:

$$\frac{\$13,200}{24} = \$550$$

82. B: Rearrange the equation to isolate the variable:

$$13 + x = 130$$
$$x = 130 - 13$$
$$x = 117$$

83. D: Recall that, for a rectangle, area (A) is length (l) times width (w):

$$A = l \times w$$
$$= 10 \text{ ft} \times 15 \text{ ft}$$
$$= 150 \text{ ft}^2$$

84. B: To solve, first find what percent of the paycheck is taken out: 30% + 15% + 32% = 77%. Subtract this number from 100% to find out the amount of her paycheck that is remaining: 23%.

85. D: To solve this problem, first figure our Dale's new rate by multiplying 45 by 0.07 (7% as a decimal) and adding this to his original rate ($45).

$$\$45 \times 0.07 + \$45 = \$3.15 + \$45 = \$48.15$$

Then, determine how many hours he would have worked last year to earn $135. Do this by dividing $135 by his hourly wage ($45).

$$\$135 \div \$45/\text{hr} = 3 \text{ hrs}$$

Finally, multiply his new hourly wage ($48.15) by 3 to figure out how much he would have earned for the same project this year.

$$\$48.15 \times 3 = \$144.45$$

86. A: Divide 17 by 20 to get 0.85. Convert 0.85 into a percentage by multiplying by 100%, essentially moving the decimal two places to the right.

87. C: Since they are on a straight line, these angles all add up to 180°, which is the measure of a straight line. The two stated angles add up to 120°, so the third angle on this line is 60°.

88. A: To solve, move the decimal left (since the scientific notation has a negative power) 6 places.

89. D: To solve, add the increase in her measurement to her present height:

$$3' \, 8" + 5" = 4' \, 1"$$

Now subtract that new height from her mother's height to find out how much more she will have to grow:

$$5' \, 1" - 4' \, 1" = 1' = 12"$$

90. A: Multiply 60 mph by 15 hours to find out how far he drove on Day 1:

$$60 \text{ mph} \times 15 \text{ hr} = 900 \text{ mi}$$

If he does the same on Day 2, he will have driven a total of 1,800 miles. He will have 200 miles left to go on a 2,000-mile trip.

91. B: To solve, first figure out how much money she put down:

$$\$125{,}000 \times 22\% = \$27{,}500$$

Subtract the down payment from the original price:

$$\$125{,}000 - \$27{,}500 = \$97{,}500$$

92. B: To solve, place the value of x into the equation:

$$y = -\frac{1}{2} + 4$$
$$y = 3\frac{1}{2}$$

93. C: To solve, first figure out how many messages he had this month: $35 + 48 = 83$. Subtract this from the amount he gets each month: $83 - 50 = 33$. Multiply these extra messages by 15 cents: $33 \times \$0.15 = \$4.95$. Add the monthly fee: $\$4.95 + \$7.00 = \$11.95$.

94. C: To order these numbers, first order the negative numbers from least to greatest. Remember, the largest negative number is the smallest.

$$-1.32, -0.42$$

Then, 0 will separate the negative numbers from the positive numbers.

Finally, order the positive numbers from least to greatest.

$$0.014, 0.308, 0.31$$

The numbers ordered from least to greatest are: $-1.32, -0.42, 0, 0.014, 0.308, 0.31$.

95. C: Choose two angles that take up the entire line, since a straight line has a measure of 180°.

96. B: To solve, isolate y on one side of the equation:

$$4y = 60 - 16$$
$$4y = 44$$
$$y = 11$$

97. D: To solve, first multiply it out:

$$3(x - 12) - 11 - 3(x - 4) = 3x - 36 - 11 - 3x + 12$$

Positive and negative $3x$ cancel each other out, leaving:

$$-36 - 11 + 12 = -35$$

98. B: To solve, first convert 25% to a decimal: 0.25. Then, multiply 160 by 0.25 to get 40.

99. B: To solve, divide the numerator by the denominator and multiply by 100:

$$\frac{42}{7} \times 100 = 6 \times 100 = 600\%$$

100. D: To divide fractions, multiply the divisor (the second fraction) by its reciprocal (turn it upside down). Then, reduce or simplify the fraction:

$$\frac{2}{5} \times \frac{3}{2} = \frac{6}{10} = \frac{3}{5}$$

101. A: Out of the twenty students in the classroom, half are girls. That means there is a 1 in 2, or 50%, chance that the homework handed in will belong to a girl.

102. C: To solve, isolate x by rearranging the equation:

$$2x - 6 + 4x = 24$$
$$6x - 6 = 24$$
$$6x = 30$$
$$x = 5$$

103. A: To convert a percentage into a decimal, move the decimal two places to the left and remove the percent sign: $22\% = 0.22$

104. C: To solve, find the perimeter (the distance around the outside) of each by adding the length of each side of the rectangles:

Garden A: 4 ft by 9 ft rectangle, 4 ft + 9 ft + 4 ft + 9 ft = 26 ft

Garden B: 12 ft by 3 ft rectangle, 12 ft + 3 ft + 12 ft + 3 ft = 30 ft

Garden C: 18 ft by 2 ft rectangle, 18 ft + 2 ft + 18 ft + 2 ft = 40 ft

The largest perimeter, Garden C, will require the most fencing.

105. B: Since $\overleftrightarrow{AB}$ is a straight line (its measure is 180°) and $\angle ADC = 45°$:

$$\angle BDC = 180° - 45° = 135°$$

106. D: An equilateral triangle means that all sides are the same length.

107. C: We know that ΔDEF is a right triangle, but we don't know whether the hypotenuse is $\overline{EF}$ or $\overline{DF}$. If $\overline{EF}$ is the hypotenuse, $\overline{DF}$ is calculated the Pythagorean theorem:

$$8^2 = 6^2 + b^2$$
$$64 - 36 = b^2$$
$$28 = b^2$$
$$\sqrt{28} = b$$

Since the square root of 28 is not one of the choices, we must consider $\overline{DF}$ to be the hypotenuse. In this case:

$$c^2 = 6^2 + 8^2$$
$$c^2 = 36 + 64$$
$$c^2 = 100$$
$$c = 10$$

108. D: To solve, convert the pounds to ounces (one pound is 16 oz): a quarter-pound of blueberries equals 4 oz; a half-pound of strawberries equals 8 oz; a half-pound of yogurt equals 8 oz, a quarter-pound of walnuts equals 4 oz.

$$4\text{ oz} + 8\text{ oz} + 8\text{ oz} + 4\text{ oz} = 24\text{ oz}$$

$$20\text{ oz} \times \frac{\$0.15}{\text{oz}} = \$3.60$$

109. B: Factors are numbers that when multiplied together provide the result. Zero is not a factor of any number. The numbers 1, 2, 3, and 4 are all factors of 12.

110. C: This question requires two steps. The first step is to determine the discounted earring price by multiplying $500 by 0.75 (75%, the amount that isn't taken off from the discount, as a decimal).

$$\$500 \times 0.75 = \$375$$

The second step is to use the birthday discount. With the birthday discount, she will still pay 95% (100%-5%) of the discounted price, so multiply $375 by 0.95.

$$\$375 \times 0.95 = \$356.25$$

Since this is Mary's birthday month, she pays $356.25 for the pair of earrings.

111. B: Multiply the numerators and the denominators and then simplify:

$$\frac{3}{4} \times \frac{4}{5} = \frac{3 \times 4}{4 \times 5} = \frac{12}{20} = \frac{3}{5}$$

112. A: To determine how many students will be absent, multiply the percentage of students who will be absent by the total number of students.

$$8\% \times 452 = 0.08 \times 452 = 36.16$$

Therefore, about 36 students will be absent on April 20.

113. C: Similar figures have a proportional shape but not necessarily the same size and congruent figures are exactly the same. These two figures are neither.

114. D: To solve, first figure out how much money Tim has earned just for child care, then determine the bonus amount, and then add in the bonus amount:

$$childcare = 4 \text{ hours} \times \frac{\$5.00}{\text{hour}} = \$20.00$$

$$bonus = \$20.00 \times 0.20 = \$4.00$$

$$total = \$20.00 + \$4.00 = \$24.00$$

115. C: Analyze each option to see if it can be further reduced. $\frac{6}{50}$ can be reduced to $\frac{3}{25}$ by dividing the numerator and denominator by 2, so it is not in lowest terms. $\frac{12}{100}$ can be reduced to $\frac{3}{25}$ by dividing the numerator and denominator by 4, so it is not in lowest terms. $\frac{12}{10}$ can be reduced to $\frac{6}{5}$ or $1\frac{1}{5}$ by dividing the numerator and denominator by 2, so it is not in lowest terms. $\frac{11}{5}$ can be rewritten as $2\frac{1}{5}$, so it is not in lowest terms. $\frac{3}{25}$ is the only fraction that cannot be simplified or rewritten as a mixed number, so it is the correct answer.

116. B: To determine how much Brenda would have saved, first find out the sale price of the shoes and then subtract this price from the amount Brenda paid. The sale price of the shoes is:

$$\$62 \times 0.75 = \$46.50$$

Then, subtract this amount from the amount Brenda paid:

$$\$62 - \$46.50 = \$15.50$$

Brenda would have saved $15.50 if she had waited a day.

117. B: A is a number in the thousandths. B, C, and D are in tenths. Three-tenths (0.300) is the largest of these choices.

118. D: All the options except for 7 can be multiplied by another whole number to equal 870.

Thank You

We at Mometrix would like to extend our heartfelt thanks to you, our friend and patron, for allowing us to play a part in your journey. It is a privilege to serve people from all walks of life who are unified in their commitment to building the best future they can for themselves.

The preparation you devote to these important testing milestones may be the most valuable educational opportunity you have for making a real difference in your life. We encourage you to put your heart into it—that feeling of succeeding, overcoming, and yes, conquering will be well worth the hours you've invested.

We want to hear your story, your struggles and your successes, and if you see any opportunities for us to improve our materials so we can help others even more effectively in the future, please share that with us as well. **The team at Mometrix would be absolutely thrilled to hear from you!** So please, send us an email (support@mometrix.com) and let's stay in touch.

If you feel as though you need additional help, please check out the other resources we offer:

Study Guide: http://MometrixStudyGuides.com/CEOE

Flashcards: http://MometrixFlashcards.com/CEOE